Alain Robbe-Grillet

Manchester University Press

DIANA HOLMES and ROBERT INGRAM *series editors*
DUDLEY ANDREW *series consultant*

FRENCH FILM DIRECTORS

Alain Robbe-Grillet

JOHN PHILLIPS

Manchester University Press

MANCHESTER AND NEW YORK

distributed in the United States exclusively by Palgrave Macmillan

Published by Manchester University Press
Oxford Road, Manchester M13 9NR, UK
and Room 400, 175 Fifth Avenue, New York, NY 10010, USA
www.manchesteruniversitypress.co.uk

Distributed exclusively in the USA by
Palgrave, 175 Fifth Avenue, New York, NY 10010, USA

Distributed exclusively in Canada by
UBC Press, University of British Columbia, 2029 West Mall, Vancouver, BC, Canada v6T 1Z2

British Library Cataloguing-in-Publication Data
A catalogue record for this book is available from the British Library

Library of Congress Cataloging-in-Publication Data applied for

ISBN 978 0 7190 7737 1 *hardback*

First published 2011

Typeset in Scala with Meta display
by Koinonia, Manchester
Printed in Great Britain
by the MPG Books Group, UK

Contents

List of plates

Series editors' foreword

To an anglophone audience, the combination of the words 'French' and 'cinema' evokes a particular kind of film: elegant and wordy, sexy but serious – an image as dependent upon national stereotypes as is that of the crudely commercial Hollywood blockbuster, which is not to say that either image is without foundation. Over the past two decades, this generalised sense of a significant relationship between French identity and film has been explored in scholarly books and articles, and has entered the curriculum at university level and, in Britain, at A-level. The study of film as art-form and (to a lesser extent) as industry, has become a popular and widespread element of French Studies, and French cinema has acquired an important place within Film Studies. Meanwhile, the growth in multi-screen and 'art-house' cinemas, together with the development of the video industry, has led to the greater availability of foreign-language films to an English-speaking audience. Responding to these developments, this series is designed for students and teachers seeking information and accessible but rigorous critical study of French cinema, and for the enthusiastic filmgoer who wants to know more.

The adoption of a director-based approach raises questions about auteurism. A series that categorises films not according to period or to genre (for example), but to the person who directed them, runs the risk of espousing a romantic view of film as the product of solitary inspiration. On this model, the critic's role might seem to be that of discovering continuities, revealing a necessarily coherent set of themes and motifs which correspond to the particular genius of the individual. This is not our aim: the auteur perspective on film, itself most clearly articulated in France in the early 1950s, will be interrogated in certain volumes of the series, and, throughout, the director will be treated as one highly significant element in a complex process of film production and reception which includes socio-economic and political determinants, the work of a large and highly skilled team of artists and technicians, the mechanisms of production and distribution, and the complex and multiply determined responses of spectators.

The work of some of the directors in the series is already well known outside France, that of others is less so – the aim is both to provide informative and original English-language studies of established figures, and to extend the range of French directors known to anglophone students of cinema. We intend the series to contribute to the promotion of the formal and informal study of French films, and to the pleasure of those who watch them.

DIANA HOLMES
ROBERT INGRAM

Acknowledgements

I gratefully acknowledge the assistance of the following in granting permission for the inclusion in my book of poster and still images from the films:

Catherine Robbe-Grillet and the estate of Alain Robbe-Grillet;
L'IMEC;
Laurence Tremolet (for permission to print the photograph taken during the shooting of *Un bruit qui rend fou*);
Argos Films (for permission to print the poster for *L'Année dernière à Marienbad*).

In addition, my heartfelt thanks to Diana Holmes, the series editor who read my manuscript and made excellent suggestions for improvement, to Matthew Frost and everyone at Manchester University Press.

Introduction

My books were not real novels, but sort of failed films, aborted films.
Robbe-Grillet, *Préface à une vie d'écrivain*

Alain Robbe-Grillet was born in Brest in 1922. Having studied agronomy and worked as a research biologist for a number of years in Africa and the French Caribbean, he began to write novels in the late 1940s, and film scripts a decade later. He died suddenly of a heart attack in February 2008, leaving behind a corpus of eleven novels, four 'romanesques', or creative autobiographies, essays on the novel, photography and sculpture, and a not insubstantial corpus of films. He scripted a total of eleven films, all but one of which he also directed. In spite of his claim that his work ended in 1996 (Waters 2000: 189), his artistic career therefore spanned six decades, and his novelistic work has had a profound impact in literary circles, although this intellectual influence has not always been matched by public acclaim. While his cinema has attracted numerous awards, and has been the subject of many international film festivals (such as the ten-day-long festival of his films held at the Institut Français in London in 1996), they have not attracted the same amount of attention in the English-speaking world as his novels.[1] This is partly due to a general reluctance on the part of English speakers to view French films, but there may be other reasons for this neglect, including a growing erotic, and some might claim, pornographic content.[2] Whatever the truth of such claims, it is one of the main aims of this book to demonstrate that, both in

---

1 'In the Temple of Dreams: The Writer on the Screen (The Complete Films of Alain Robbe-Grillet)', French Institute, London, 18–28 September 1996.
2 The 'pornography' question will be considered in detail in Chapter 5.

terms of the innovative qualities of the work and the influence he has exerted on other film-makers and artists, Robbe-Grillet's contribution to the cinema deserves the same degree of critical attention as that accorded to his novels.

It is as *chef de file* of the French New Novel movement that Robbe-Grillet came to public attention in the 1950s, his first novel, *Les Gommes* (*The Erasers*), published in 1953 by Les Éditions de Minuit, the small publishing house of which he was the literary director, attracting considerable interest in Parisian intellectual circles, if not among the wider public. With the exception of Marguerite Duras, who always remained on the fringes of the movement both artistically and in more concrete ways, the New Novelists have never won a mainstream readership, but they have exerted an undeniable influence on theories of novel-writing and of artistic representation in general. Both Duras and Robbe-Grillet extended their work into the cinema in the early 1960s, and to a limited degree their respective careers ran along parallel tracks throughout that decade.[3] Duras's filmic work consists of a number of experimental projects in collaboration with established film-makers such as Alain Resnais and on her own account, by far her best known and arguably most artistically satisfying contribution to the genre being the iconic *Hiroshima mon amour* (1959) which she scripted and Resnais directed. Robbe-Grillet's first foray into cinema was also a collaboration with Resnais, *L'année dernière à Marienbad* (1961), a film that has achieved an equally iconic status. Resnais directed *Marienbad*, but the initial idea was Robbe-Grillet's and the script was his. The question of the film's paternity will be addressed in Chapter 1.

There is thus a discernible synchronicity in the work of at least two major figures on the intellectual scene of the 1960s, which argues for a certain historical rootedness, and indeed, some critics have made a plausible case for reading both Duras and Robbe-Grillet as emerging from a very specific historical context, readings which to some degree appear to militate against the claims of the New Novel school to have evacuated all historical or political elements in their quest for art forms expressing internal rather than external forms of reality. It is worth stressing here that such readings may form part of a wider approach to Robbe-Grillet, according to which the work

3 Julia Waters (2000) has argued that the parallels are considerably more extensive, relating to theme and form, as well as to choice of genre.

may sometimes be read against its author, and this approach will be considered in the following chapters, especially in Chapter 4. A brief overview of the entire filmic corpus and its critical reception will help the reader to gain an approximate view of his status and importance as a film-maker before we look more closely at the films and their themes and forms.

Critical reception

After *Marienbad*, Robbe-Grillet made his directorial debut with *L'Immortelle* (1963). This film was not well received by most reviewers, as Robbe-Grillet himself recalls in an essay written in the year of the film's release, 'Temps et description dans le récit d'aujourd'hui'.[4] Predictably, he notes, the actors' performance was criticised as being 'unnatural', critics bemoaned the difficulty of distinguishing between what was 'real' and what was memory or fantasy, and disliked the tendency to stereotype both the city of Istanbul and the emotions of the characters (ibid.:129). What all these criticisms boiled down to, in his view, was the absence of 'objective truth'. His response provides a summation of the entire basis of the 'new cinema':

> toute œuvre moderne [...] au lieu d'être un prétendu morceau de réalité, se développe en tant que réflexion sur la réalité (ou sur le *peu de réalité* comme on voudra). Elle ne cherche plus à cacher son caractère nécessairement mensonger, en se présentant comme une «histoire vécue». Si bien que nous retrouvons là, dans l'écriture cinématographique, une fonction voisine de celle assumée par la description en littérature: l'image ainsi traîtée [*sic*] (quant aux acteurs, au décor, au montage, dans ses rapports avec le son, etc.) empêche de croire en même temps qu'elle affirme, comme la description empêchait de voir ce qu'elle montrait.[5] (ibid.: 129–30)

4 Robbe-Grillet 1963c: 123–34.
5 'any modern work [...] rather than being presented as a slice of real life, is constructed as a reflection on reality (or on the *lack of reality* if you wish). It no longer seeks to hide its necessarily mendacious character, as the presentation of a "real story". The result is that the filmic text functions in a similar manner to that of the literary description: treated in this way (as regards actors, set, editing, sound, etc.) the image prevents the spectator from believing at the same time as it affirms itself, just as literary description prevented us from seeing what it showed.' This and all subsequent translations in the book are my own, unless otherwise stated.

René Prédal argues that it was not the case that Robbe-Grillet's films were very poorly received – Prédal cites a number of glowing reviews in the French press – but reactions, often prompted by Robbe-Grillet's own interventions in the critical debate, were complex.[6] Prédal points out that the 1960s were the golden age of film magazines in France, the most popular being *Cinéma* and *Image et Son*, though the most famous were *Les Cahiers du cinéma* and *Positif*, the latter two able to make and break reputations and leading the theoretical debate: 'Gare aux cinéastes excommuniés par *Les Cahiers*, surtout s'ils ne sont pas récupérés à *Positif!* Or c'est exactement la mésaventure qui arrive à Robbe-Grillet qui n'a jamais été apprécié ni par l'une ni par l'autre des publications'[7] (Prédal 2005: 93). No *Cahiers* critic wrote a long review that was favourable. Jacques Doniol-Valcroze, the then editor-in-chief, was one of the few critics of the time to understand what *L'Immortelle* was about: 'remplacement du référent extérieur par une réalité intrinsèque au film, perpétuel présent du temps mental d'un narrateur qui n'interprète pas mais se raconte lui-même une histoire nourrie de fantasmes'[8] (1963: 143; quoted by Prédal, ibid.).

Robbe-Grillet's next film, *Trans-Europ-Express* (1966) suffered a worse fate at the hands of the critics who were generally hostile to the film's erotic character. The editor-in-chief of *Image et Son* published a long and entirely negative review of the film: 'petit film médiocre et prétentieux [...] tourné par un amateur incapable de conduire un récit filmique'[9] (Chevassu 1967: 203). As Prédal acutely observes, 'Décidément Robbe-Grillet dérange!'[10] (2005: 97).With *L'Homme qui ment* (1968), on the other hand, critics were more divided, Dominique Noguez, for instance, calling the film a 'Marienbad without Resnais', while Doniol-Valcroze underlined the radicality of an author-director

---

6 The following summary owes much to René Prédal's invaluable survey of the films' critical reception (2005: 91–104). Prédal focuses on specialised film magazines.

7 'Woe betide those film-makers excommunicated by *Les Cahiers*, especially if they are not rescued by *Positif!* Now, this was precisely the misfortune that befell Robbe-Grillet who has never been appreciated by either of these publications.'

8 'the replacement of an external referent by a reality intrinsic to the film itself, the perpetual present of the psychological time of a narrator who does not interpret but tells himself a story filled with fantasies'

9 'a mediocre and pretentious little film [...] shot by an amateur incapable of putting a film together'

10 'Robbe-Grillet was clearly making waves!'

who questioned the nature of reality (see Prédal 2005: 95). In the late 1960s, Robbe-Grillet's films suffered to some degree from the growing leftist focus of *Les Cahiers,* especially in the wake of May 1968. This was no time for the evacuation of the referent!

Positif either completely ignored Robbe-Grillet's films or allocated a few negative comments to them in the magazine's 'A to Z' section. Michel Grisolia in *Positif* condemned *L'Eden et après* (1971) as a 'bric-à-brac usé provoquant l'ennui'[11] (1970: 118). As for *Glissements progressifs du plaisir* (1974), 'Robbe-Grillet, c'est l'homme qui ment'[12] (Bolduc 1975: 167).[13] Alain Garsault was similarly negative about *Le Jeu avec le feu* (1974; see Prédal 2005: 96). All these adverse reactions are to be explained in terms of the ultra-conservative position of *Positif* in the 1960s, a journal that rejected any innovative approaches, having already condemned the entire *nouvelle vague. La Saison cinématographique,* on the other hand (an annual publication of reviews of all the films appearing on French cinema screens from 1 January to 31 December) judged none of Robbe-Grillet's films negatively (despite the fact that the team writing them was made up of the same editors as *Image et Son*). Raymond Lefèvre, writing for this magazine, singled out *Trans-Europ-Express* for its qualities which he listed *inter alia* as a reworking of the traditional narrative, the deconstruction of the notion of character, and an attack on clichés and stereotypes (ibid.: 98).

Gradually, then, individual critics rebelled against the magazine's hegemony. Noël Burch, for example, wrote some very subtle things in 1967 about *Marienbad* and *L'Immortelle.* Burch and Labarthe made several TV programmes together for the prestigious series, *Cinéastes de notre temps,* produced by Labarthe and Janine Bazin (1964–72), one of which was devoted to Robbe-Grillet in 1969. Prédal lists a number of other magazines and networks of admirers of Robbe-Grillet's films: *Télé Ciné, L'Avant-Scène Cinéma,* etc. (ibid.: 99). But it was above all *Cinéma,* founded in 1954, which has most consistently supported Robbe-Grillet, in particular, his first two films. *L'Immortelle* was very positively received in this magazine, and *Trans-Europ-Express* was rated a masterpiece (March 1967: 114). *Glissements,* however, was not well received in *Cinéma* (March 1974: 185), but the following year, *Le*

11 'a worn-out antique generating boredom'
12 'The man who lies is Robbe-Grillet'
13 Albert Bolduc does not exist, this being a pseudonym of the editorial committee.

Jeu avec le feu (1975) was defended for its technical mastery, humour and playfulness (April 1975: 197).

In the next quarter century, Robbe-Grillet made only two films, *La Belle captive* (1983) and *Un bruit qui rend fou* (1995). Both suffered at the hands of *Positif* and *Cahiers* reviewers. The latter film, for instance, was condemned in *Les Cahiers* as 'sans surprise, plein de passé'[14] (1995: 496).

In academic circles, the warmth with which his films have been received has generally depended on the theoretical perspective of the critic. In the 1960s, structuralists such as the early Roland Barthes tended to play down the sexually disturbing elements of the work to focus on it as text, divorced from any social or political reality. On the other hand, even early films such as *L'Immortelle*, which cannot be said to contain any explicit sexual references, attracted a degree of negative criticism from morally minded critics, as evidenced in what came to be known as 'la querelle du *Voyeur*' (Waters 2000: 58–9). Such critics constituted a growing number from the 1970s onwards, as Robbe-Grillet's novelistic and cinematic work began to make those hitherto muted themes of perversion and sadomasochism increasingly explicit. That such criticism already existed in the 1950s is evident from Barthes's defence of *Le Voyeur* against the charge of obscenity. Barthes retaliated by characterising such views as stemming from a confusion between reality and the imagination. The novel, Barthes argued, was formal experimentation, and not a symbolic expression of the real (1955: 67).

From the 1970s on, feminist critics insisted on the presence of a female body in the text, on the political and ideological implications of this presence, and the manner in which it is represented. Given the increasingly explicit eroticism of both his novels and films, Robbe-Grillet's work was especially vulnerable, of all the New Novelists and New Film-makers, to hostile feminist readings. Sadomasochistic themes and motifs are found to varying degrees of explicitness in all his films. Rape, murder, bondage, lesbianism, prostitution, the torture of naked young women, and imagery with strong fetishistic components have proved problematic for some critics, who have pointed to its personal origins in the author's own self-avowed sexual fantasies.[15] Conversely, others have repeated the authorial view that

14 'passé and lacking originality'
15 Such an intensely personal investment seems to be at odds with Roland

the female characters in his films can generally be said to stand up to male authority. Alice, in *Glissements*, resists patriarchy, as represented by the law and the church, while in *La Belle captive*, the evocatively named Sara Zeitgeist is seen to be sexually and psychologically dominant over the film's male protagonist. However, Sara, and to a lesser extent, Alice, are vulnerable to the charge of fulfilling a common male fantasy, and one certainly shared by their creator: the dominatrix. Yet, as I have argued elsewhere in relation to his novels, Robbe-Grillet's use of such material is complex, and inseparable from his experimental representation of an internal reality, informed by dreams, fantasies and nightmares (see Phillips 1999: 129–48). Moreover, the sexual is always *mis en scène* in both novels and films within an ironic frame that implicitly questions the stereotypes of sex and gender found in more conventional narratives.[16]

Such an approach is essentially ideological, and in this and other ways, the films can be said to have a political dimension in the broadest sense of the word that seems to contradict their author's aim to produce an art disengaged from a socio-historical context. My position in this regard is close to that of Lynn Higgins who has argued in relation to the New Wave cinema in general that Robbe-Grillet's films exhibit a tension between, on the one hand, a pursuit of formalism that eschews the socio-political, and on the other, implicit if not explicit responses to the sexual politics and permissiveness of the 1960s and subsequent decades (see Higgins 1996: 83–111).[17] Higgins rejects the alleged eclipse of the social in the nouveau roman and in cinema of the *nouvelle vague*, arguing that such works are inevitably shaped, even in their formal aspects, by the political events and ideas of the period (ibid.: 2). In Robbe-Grillet's case, this was in particular the climate of sexual politics that dominated the 1970s and 1980s. The films he made in those decades both take advantage of a more permissive society and contain themes that help us to understand the sexual

---

Barthes's view of the work as an exemplary case of authorless writing (see, for example, 1964, 1984).

16 See Chapters 5 and 6 for a more detailed discussion of the sexual themes and images in the films. The representation of stereotypes will also be treated in detail in Chapter 5.

17 The '*nouvelle vague*', or 'New Wave' was an avant-garde movement in French cinema, christened by François Truffaut and practised by Truffaut, Jean-Luc Godard, Eric Rohmer, Agnès Varda and others in the 1950s and 1960s. For a fuller discussion, see the beginning of Chapter 1.

politics of the time. At the same time, as Jacques Leenhardt's (1973) brilliant study of *La Jalousie* demonstrates, his works are also amenable to analysis in the context of other elements of the socio-political.[18]

Both the erotic and the historical dimensions of the films are thus vulnerable to readings running counter to Robbe-Grillet's theoretical statements. These aspects, along with the less contentious characteristics outlined above, will be considered in greater detail in relation to *Marienbad* and other films in subsequent chapters.

The polarisation of critical views has to some degree hindered objective evaluation of both novels and films, and my discussion of the filmic corpus will aim at a more measured critique which will take account of the author's own changing attitudes with regard to the exclusion of all subjective elements.

How to read Robbe-Grillet's films

Before examining the films in detail, we need to consider to what extent both the author's theories of the novel and identifiable thematic and formal currents are carried over into film-making.

It is rare for an important writer to become an equally important film-maker. However, although, as Robbe-Grillet himself has claimed, it may be possible to find common ground between the thematics of his films and those of his novels, Robbe-Grillet is not a novelist whose work is simply adapted for the screen (see Fragola and Smith 1992: 146). Why then did Robbe-Grillet make films? As in all his work, it is form and not content that is ostensibly the focus of his creativity:

> There is *nothing* I want to express. I have nothing to express. I feel like manipulating forms. I paint because plastic forms interest me. I write literature because the structure of sentences and words interest me, and I make films because the image and the sound interest me [...] I have nothing at all to express that *precedes* expression [...] Why exactly do we manipulate forms? Because certain things escape conceptualization [...] cinema is for me a way of practicing narrative without

18 Leenhardt conducts the first post-colonial reading of Robbe-Grillet's work in his ground-breaking study of the 1957 novel, *La Jalousie*. In Chapter 4, I shall argue that Robbe-Grillet's privileging of Middle Eastern and Turkish locations in three of his films irresistibly invites a post-colonial approach.

making use of words. I use relatively few words in my films [...] I am
primarily interested in images and sounds. (Ibid.: 147)[19]

When Robbe-Grillet began making films at the beginning of the
1960s, the dominant ideology in cinema was a realist one.[20] Partly
under the influence of Alain Resnais (*Hiroshima, mon amour*), and
other auteurs of the *nouvelle vague*, especially Jean-Luc Godard, whom
he admired as a great inventor of cinematographic forms, he reacted
against this ideology, according to which dreams and reality should
be clearly separated, interrogating the very notion of reality itself: is
the 'real' objective, psychological or purely constructed? Indeed, if
there is a 'reality' in the fictions of Robbe-Grillet, it is a psychological
one. The narratives of Robbe-Grillet's films, like those of his novels,
are not mirrors moving along a road, reflecting an external reality, in
accordance with the nineteenth-century novelist Stendhal's definition
of realism, but in one important sense, reflections of the very process
of storytelling. Robbe-Grillet speaks more lucidly on this point than
many of his critics, distinguishing reality from realism:

> I detest realism, that is to say, the realist illusion. Reality is not realism.
> Reality is worrisome; realism is reassuring [...] I know that I am alive
> here and now. Yet I also am aware that a great part of this life, perhaps
> its greatest part, is memory. I am concerned with man's internal
> state. I believe that the more an adventure is impassioned, the more
> it involves the imaginary. You noticed the allusion to Marcel Proust
> in (*La Belle Captive*), who in fact remarked that when a man loves a
> woman she is an imaginary woman. (Fragola and Smith 1992: 108)

Robbe-Grillet's imaginative world is very much the inner world
of dreams and the unconscious. One can easily detect here the influence of the surrealists, one which he has often acknowledged. Close
parallels have been noted, for example, between *Marienbad* and Luis
Buñuel's and Salvador Dalí's *Un Chien andalou* ('An Andalusian
Dog'), especially in their rejection of linear time (ibid.: 6). Robbe-
Grillet's debt to surrealism is also evident in the depiction of human

19 The critic, Jean Ricardou famously described the new novel in terms of an
artistic and formalistic exploration: 'Le récit n'est pas l'écriture d'une aventure,
mais l'aventure d'une écriture.' ('The narrative is not the writing of an adventure, but the adventure of writing' (*Pour une théorie du nouveau roman*).
20 In *Angélique, ou l'enchantement*, Robbe-Grillet bemoans the regressive theories
of the *Cahiers du cinéma* group which promoted Bazin's 'simplistic neo-realism':
see Robbe-Grillet 1987: 175–7.

beings as dolls or automata (as found in the works of Duchamp, Man Ray, Bellmer, Dalí, Magritte), and the doubling technique which he often employs was originally associated with Buñuel.[21] Both of these techniques undermine any tendency on the spectator's part to identify singular characters with fixed and stable identities.

This tendency away from static representations of reality, whether social or psychological, is discernible in the 'murder mystery' aspects of his films, an area in which he may owe some debt to Alfred Hitchcock who also sought to represent a reality that constantly eludes fixed identification. Other film-makers whose influence he has acknowledged include Orson Welles, and Sergei Eisenstein whose theories of sound and montage fitted in with his desire to undermine views of an objective reality by showing sight and sound as operating subjectively in the minds of his characters. His approach to montage as a succession of individual and often incongruous shots, as opposed to a coherent succession of sequences, links him to Eisenstein and the surrealists.[22] Such a cinematographic technique was highly innovative, a courageous attempt to represent the imagination and its spatio-temporal dimensions in visual terms.

Robbe-Grillet's films, *Marienbad* included, therefore constituted a major departure from the traditional realist cinema, just as the *nouveau roman* had done with regard to conventional novelistic practice. His innovative approach to both genres is rooted in the strongly held view that all art, cinema included, must challenge and disrupt, and on a philosophical level, in a strongly atheistic rejection of any form of transcendence, which he replaces with a belief in the inner world as mainspring of all human activity:

> Dans le rêve, dans le souvenir, comme dans le regard, notre imagination est la force organisatrice de notre vie. Chaque homme, à son tour, doit réinventer les choses autour de lui. Ce sont les vraies choses, nettes, dures et brillantes, du monde réel. Elles ne renvoient à aucun autre monde. Elles ne sont le signe de rien d'autre que d'elles-mêmes. Et le seul contact que l'homme puisse entretenir avec elles est de les imaginer.[23] (Robbe-Grillet 1963b: 94)

---

21 Buñuel uses this technique extensively in his films. On Buñuel's and Antonio's influence, see Robbe-Grillet (2005: 222–7). For a detailed discussion of this technique, see Chapter 2.

22 See Chapter 3 where this approach is discussed in more detail.

23 'In dream, in memory, as in the gaze, our imagination is the force that organises

This statement draws attention to his oft-repeated rejection of any meaningful connection between humans and the world they inhabit, an insistence which marks his claim to differ from the politically committed writers who preceded him such as Sartre and Camus, whose characters are inescapably engaged in a social, political and philosophical sense with the ostensible absurdity of the reality around them. In what may have been Robbe-Grillet's last public talk at the Serpentine Gallery in September 2007, he explained this idea with characteristic clarity, with the aid of a quotation from Hegel. Musing about the nature of reality and attempting to pare away all uncertainty, Hegel realised that reality and time were intimately connected, but that, as time was constantly changing, being itself was the only certainty: 'Nun ist Tag' ('Now it's day') becomes 'Nun ist Nacht' ('Now it's night'), and therefore, 'Nun ist' ('Now is', or the brute fact of existence) can be the only constant. In *Pour un nouveau roman*, Robbe-Grillet had expressed this idea with the writers of the previous generation in mind: 'Or le monde n'est ni signifiant ni absurde. Il *est*, tout simplement'[24] (1963a:18). Such a refusal to acknowledge meaningful connections at an ontological level has led him to create narrative forms that can prove rebarbative for the new reader or spectator, accustomed to realist genres. A brief consideration of how not to read the films may therefore offer the uninitiated an accessible way in.

First, and most important of all, there is nothing to be gained in trying to identify a conventional plot. The New Novel and the new cinema in its wake are focused on formal experimentation with little or no regard for the telling of a conventional story. Robbe-Grillet opposes the more profound, inner reality to the artificial construction of a social backcloth against which characters move and act according to the *trompe-l'œil* laws of psychological realism. The Real, on the other hand, in the psychoanalytical sense of that word, is omnipresent in Robbe-Grillet's films, not least in the images of cutting, of blood and broken bottles, that keep washing up on the shores of his imaginary. For Slavoj Žižek, who relies on Lacanian theories of the Real, 'cutting is a radical attempt to (re)gain a hold on reality [...] to ground the ego

---

our lives. Each individual, in their turn, must reinvent the objects around him. These are the real things, clear, hard and shiny, of the real world. They do not relate to any other world. They are not signs of anything other than themselves. And the only contact that man can maintain with them is to imagine them.'

24 'The world is neither meaningful nor absurd, it just is'

firmly in bodily reality, against the unbearable anxiety of perceiving oneself as non-existent [...] so although, of course, cutting is a pathological phenomenon, it is nonetheless a pathological attempt at regaining some kind of normality, at avoiding a total psychotic breakdown' (2002: 10).

While Robbe-Grillet is much closer to this 'Real' than to any conventional conception of realism, he stresses at the same time that he is a creator, not a transcriber of reality, as indeed are all human beings: 'Chaque homme, à son tour, doit réinventer les choses autour de lui'[25] (1963b: 94). The reader/spectator needs to play an active, conscious and creative role: 'Car, loin de le négliger, l'auteur aujourd'hui proclame l'absolu besoin qu'il a de son concours, un concours actif, conscient, *créateur* [...] il lui demande [...] de participer à une création, d'inventer à son tour l'œuvre – et le monde – et d'apprendre ainsi à inventer sa propre vie'[26] (Robbe-Grillet 1963c: 134). This explains why his novels and films have been compared to puzzles and detective stories, although in his case there are no answers or solutions. Robbe-Grillet stresses the importance of doubt, and that the 'reality' of his fictions is like shifting sands, so that the stories of his novels and films often contain repetitions of a single scene but with slight variations. In *Le Voyeur*, for example, Mathias's alibis keep changing, while in *Marienbad*, the 'rape' scene is seen from different points of view, though no single one is preferred by the narrative.

Second, Robbe-Grillet's rejection of realism necessarily leads to a different conception of time and space. The notion of realism in the nineteenth century was in conformity with the science of that period, while the physics of Einstein and of quantum mechanics in the twentieth century has led to views of reality as less certain, more fluid, dependent even on the subjective consciousness that observes it.[27] This new science is intimately related to a new conception of the human and to artistic depictions of it, as represented in Robbe-Grillet's work:

25 'Every man, in his turn, must reinvent the things around him'
26 'For, far from neglecting him, today's author proclaims the absolute need he has of his cooperation, an active, conscious, *creative* cooperation [...] he asks him [...] to participate in creation, to invent the work in his turn – and the world with it – and in the process, to learn to invent his own life.'
27 Heisenberg's now well-known principle of uncertainty, for example.

the search for a modern narrative [...] would begin by treating time differently, refusing [...] a linear unidirectional and reassuring time, that is contrary to all of contemporary thought. [...] My background is not literary but scientific, and as you know, the concept of time such as it exists in contemporary science has nothing in common with the absolute certainties of Balzac's era [...] the very notion of man itself has changed [...] the very idea of something solid and definitive has disappeared from the world. The notion of Truth, the notion of Totality, the notion of Man, all of this has collapsed. (Robbe-Grillet, quoted by Gardies 2005: 117–19)

Both the new science and our conceptions of reality are therefore dependent on theories of time and our relationship to it. As Gilles Deleuze clearly saw, Robbe-Grillet's conceptions of the sights and sounds that make up our perceptions of this reality are intimately linked to Einsteinian theories of time and space as related. Hence, Robbe-Grillet's approach to representations in film as in the novel is inevitably determined in large part by a theory of time as relative, non-chronological and measurable in isolated moments rather than in sustained, unidirectional sequences: 'Ici l'espace détruit le temps, et le temps sabote l'espace. La description piétine, se contredit, tourne en rond. L'instant nie la continuité'[28] (Robbe-Grillet 1963c: 133). In Robbe-Grillet's films, this is the time in our heads, not the linear construction of time we are used to in realist cinema. Time in his fictions has a definite presence, but it is cut off from 'temporality' in the sense of a continuous thread:

Or, si la temporalité comble l'attente, l'instantanéité la déçoit; de même que la discontinuité spatiale *déprend* du piège de l'anecdote [...] ce présent qui s'invente [...] qui se répète, se dédouble, se modifie, se dément, sans jamais s'entasser pour constituer un passé – donc une «histoire» au sens traditionnel – tout cela ne peut que convier le lecteur (ou le spectateur) à un autre mode de participation que celui dont il avait l'habitude.[29] (Ibid.: 133–4)

28 'Here space destroys time and time sabotages space. Description gets nowhere, contradicts itself, goes round in circles. The moment undermines continuity.'

29 'Now, if temporality fulfils our expectations, instantaneity disappoints them; in the same way, spatial discontinuity frees itself from the trap of the traditional story [...] that present which invents itself [...] which repeats, multiplies, modifies, contradicts itself without ever solidifying to constitute a past – hence a story in the traditional sense – all of this must compel the reader (or spectator) to participate in the narrative in a way that is different from usual'.

This conception of time not only runs counter to any concept of time as linear, it is also closer to the time of dream and of the irrational, which takes us back to Robbe-Grillet's conceptions of the real:

> Yes, and in an even more general way, it is outside the rational. When it is a question of space, it is an irrational space; when it is a question of time, it is an irrational time. Film interests me because of its possibility of exploring the irrational. All the cinematographic codes that have been invented ever since sound was added to film seem to want to re-establish the omnipotence of the rational [...] the effects of montage have a considerable possibility of creating irrational spaces. (Fragola and Smith 1992: 133–4)

Deleuze (1983) has outlined three principal ways in which the innovations of Robbe-Grillet's novelistic practice translated themselves onto the cinema screen: the privileging of the visual, which leads to a predominance of visual descriptiveness, a visual subjectivity and a purity of the visual image, untainted by any form of political or social commitment. These three characteristics of the visual, which are so clearly related in importance to cinema, are also closely related to space–time dimensions in which the new cinema makes particular innovations. As Deleuze points out, in representing technologies that make it possible to jump space–time dimensions, such as cars (*L'Immortelle*), trains (*Trans-Europ-Express*), motorbikes (*La Belle captive*), or alternatively to freeze them, as with the mirror (*Marienbad*) and camera (*Glissements*), Robbe-Grillet's cinema engages directly with the relationship between the two dimensions and with the ways in which this relationship influences our perception of reality.

Third, traditional character psychology is entirely absent. Consequently, the representation of character is rarely identifiable in his films as fully rounded. In what is often known as the Balzacian novel, for instance, proper names are an essential indicator of character, their social status and sometimes their psychological characteristics. In the nouveau roman and cinéma, proper names are frequently absent – a character may, for example, be designated by a single letter. This is the case in *Marienbad*, in *L'Immortelle*, in *L'Eden*, in *N. a pris les dés*, and also in Robbe-Grillet's best-known novel, *La Jalousie*. Similarly, the behaviour of these characters is rarely amenable to analysis in terms of a readily identifiable motivation.[30]

---

30 Grant E. Kaiser notes that, in *Marienbad*, facial expressions, normally an

Fourth and last, the discourse of the narrative is similarly resistant to conventional analysis. In linguistic terms, the act of enunciation is frequently of greater importance than the enounced, the process of speaking more significant than the words spoken. The silences of the text, too, can be more meaningful than the utterances surrounding them. In Robbe-Grillet's films, as in all cinematic work, the visual dimension plays a major role in the creation of meaning, but this is equally the case in his novels. In both genres, it is not so much action, but expression, whether visual or verbal, that really counts. This concentration on form leads to a considerable degree of self-reflexivity.

Scripts and cine-novels

One further consideration needs to be mentioned in relation to the reading of the films. Unusually and perhaps uniquely, Robbe-Grillet published what he termed a 'cinéroman' (cine-novel) in the case of four of his films: *L'Année dernière à Marienbad* (1961), *L'Immortelle* (1963d), *Glissements progressifs du plaisir* (1974) and *C'est Gradiva qui vous appelle* (2002).[31] This was a detailed but non-technical shooting-script, a genre largely of his own invention. The term is difficult to define or classify since in each case, its status and timing have been different: not so much a script, as a lengthy, detailed description in prose of the film's projected scenes, the genre was precisely defined by the author:

> Le livre qu'on va lire ne prétend pas être une œuvre par lui-même. L'œuvre, c'est le film, tel qu'on peut le voir et l'entendre dans un cinéma. On n'en trouvera ici qu'une description: ce que serait, pour un opéra, par exemple, le livret accompagné de la partition musicale et des indications de décor, et jeu, etc. [...] pour celui qui n'a pas assisté au spectacle, le cinéroman peut aussi se lire comme se lit une partition de musique.[32] (Robbe-Grillet 2005b: 7–8)

---

important indicator of character psychology, are lacking, the film focusing less on the individual psychology of love than on the process itself (1974: 119).

31 Though not strictly speaking a *cinéroman*, *La Belle captive* (Paris: Bibliothèque des Arts, 1976) was published as a 'picto-roman', with illustrations by René Magritte, seven years before the film was made.

32 'The book you are about to read does not claim to be a work in its own right. This work is the film which can be seen and heard in a cinema. All you will find here is a description, which is not unlike the script, musical score and stage

This definition, which compares the *cinéroman* to a musical score, unambiguously states, then, that the real work is the completed film. Robbe-Grillet wrote this in 1963, two years after *Marienbad* came out, and this distinction must equally apply to that film, in which case Resnais is acknowledged as the more important partner in its creation. However, he goes on to make a further distinction which appears, to some degree, to redress the balance: 'La communication doit alors passer par *l'intelligence du lecteur*, alors que l'œuvre s'adresse d'abord à *sa sensibilité* immédiate, que rien ne peut vraiment remplacer'[33] (ibid.: 8; my emphasis). In this definition, Robbe-Grillet's cinematic work takes two concomitant generic forms: the film is aimed at the sensibilities of the spectator, the *cinéroman* at the intelligence of the reader. As Corpet and Lambert point out (Robbe-Grillet 2005b: 11), Robbe-Grillet's frequent use of the term, 'récit cinématographique' (cinematic narrative) for film is equally revealing: he thus considers his work for the cinema as possessing a dual identity.

The publication of the fourth *cinéroman*, *C'est Gradiva qui vous appelle* (2002), alone pre-dates the making of the film (2006), therefore, and as such, contains no stills from it. The *Marienbad cinéroman*, though not published until shortly after the making of the film, was written in advance as a potential film project, or 'découpage' (storyboard), 'c'est-à-dire la description du film image par image tel que je le voyais dans ma tête'[34] (Robbe-Grillet 1961: 10–11), and is, in its author's own words, 'le texte [...] qui fut remis à Resnais avant le tournage'[35] (ibid.: 18), a very precise set of instructions relating to all aspects of the shooting process, together with all dialogues, but by Robbe-Grillet's own admission, work done by an author inexperienced in the making of films: 'On trouvera peu de termes techniques dans ces pages et peut-être les indications de montage, de cadrage, de mouvement d'appareil, feront sourire les spécialistes. C'est que je n'étais pas un spécialiste moi-même et que j'écrivais pour la première fois un découpage de cinéma'[36] (ibid.: 19).

directions, etc. of an opera [...] for those who have not attended the performance, the cine-novel may also be read in the same way that one reads a musical score.'

33 'The written text must therefore pass through *the reader's intelligence*, whereas the work addresses itself first and foremost to *his or her senses* which nothing can truly replace.'

34 'that is, the description of the film image by image as I saw it in my head'

35 'the text [...] given to Resnais before filming'

36 'Few technical terms will be found in these pages, and directions relating to

The second, *L'Immortelle* (1963d), also written before filming, assumes a form more recognisably cinematographic, divided into 355 shots. The third, *Glissements progressifs du plaisir* (1974), incorporates all modifications to Robbe-Grillet's original script made during the filming process.[37]

Robbe-Grillet himself made notes during filming, and in the case of those films for which no *cinéroman* was published (and of *Gradiva* where uniquely the *cinéroman* was published before the film was shot), the 'continuités dialoguées', or detailed scene summaries contained in *Scénarios en rose et noir* (2005b) are the closest to the filmed work.[38] This evolving nature of Robbe-Grillet's cinematic œuvre sharply distinguishes it from his literary work:

> Quand je rédige un projet de film [...] j'écris cette fois très vite et avec fort peu de ratures. Dans ce manuscrit-là, il s'agit seulement [...] de me faire comprendre par les nombreux collaborateurs [...] qui m'entourent pendant le repérage, la préparation des décors et des lumières, le tournage, le montage des images et des sons, etc. Toutes mes indications sont donc là-dessus aussi précises que possible, mais elles demeurent néanmoins provisoires [...] elles seront remises en cause lors du travail sur le terrain, ne serait-ce que pour tenir compte des aléas rencontrés [...] Ma rédaction préalable n'a ainsi aucune raison de ressembler à ce que Roland Barthes, dans les années cinquante, appelait 'l'écriture'.[39] (Corpet 2001: 535–6)

As the editors of the *Scénarios en rose et noir* point out, therefore, the scripts which they publish in this volume constitute a second form of cinematic writing, after the films themselves and the *cinéromans*, a sort of 'leçon de cinéma' put together during the course of the

---

staging, camera and setting may make specialists smile. The fact is that I was not a specialist myself and that I was writing a film script for the first time.'

37 Two uncompleted *cinéroman* drafts exist for *Trans-Europ-Express* (1966) and *L'Eden et après* (1971).

38 All texts published in *Scénarios* are taken from Robbe-Grillet's own archives deposited at l'IMEC, where they may be consulted: www.imec-archives.com.

39 'When I write a film proposal [...] I write very fast with few crossings-out. In this manuscript, the sole aim is to make myself understood by the many collaborators [...] who surround me during the search for a location, the building of sets and rigging of lights, the filming, the editing of images and sound track, etc. In this case, all my instructions are as precise as possible, but they nevertheless remain provisional [...] they will be open to revision during the work on the ground, if only in order to take account of unforeseen events [...] There is therefore no reason to see my first draft as what Roland Barthes in the 1950s called "écriture".'

planning and filming processes. The editors propose that all of these documents, taken together, be considered the 'cinéroman' of Robbe-Grillet's cinema as a whole (Robbe-Grillet 2005b: 15).

All of these publications may be seen as part of an attempt on the author's part, conscious or not, to fix meaning and identity.[40] They may not enjoy the status of the films themselves as objects of study, but exceptionally in this field, they allow a unique access to the genesis of the filmic work, and as such, offer valuable insights into Robbe-Grillet's creative processes. I shall therefore refer to them throughout the book.

In Chapters 2 to 6, the principal themes and motifs of the films and their technical construction will be explored in greater detail. Chapter 2 will examine the innovative manipulation of sound and vision, Chapter 3 the films' startlingly ludic qualities, Chapter 4 their love affair with orientalism, Chapter 5 the obsessive presence of the erotic. The final chapter will consider the tension that runs through all his work in the cinema between, on the one hand, a desire to improvise in collaboration with others and on the other, strong controlling tendencies on the part of an author-director with a set of powerful personal agendas, tendencies of which the publications referred to above provide some evidence.

Given the book's largely thematic approach, films may be discussed in these chapters out of chronological sequence and more than once in different contexts. First, however, we need to give special attention to this New Novelist's initial active engagement with the third art in writing the script for Alain Resnais's *L'Année dernière à Marienbad*, asking to what extent this icon of avant-garde European cinema may be considered a 'Robbe-Grillet' film, and how it prepared him for the rest of his film-making career. This, therefore, will be the subject of Chapter 1.[41]

40 The question of authorial control is the subject of Chapter 6.
41 Before Robbe-Grillet's sudden and sad demise, he had agreed to grant me an interview to take place in Paris in February 2008, ironically the month of his death. It was planned to include the text of this interview here. In place of this unforeseen omission, and because it was considered important to hear the voice of the film-maker in this unique study in English of all his films, I have drawn heavily throughout the book on existing interviews, conducted over the last thirty years, and published in *The Erotic Dream Machine* (Fragola and Smith 1992) and *Préface à une vie d'écrivain* (Robbe-Grillet 2005a). I should like to express my debt of gratitude to the editors of these collections.

References

Barthes, Roland (1955), 'Littérature littérale', in *Essais critiques*, Paris, Éditions du Seuil.

Barthes, Roland (1964), 'Il n'y a pas d'école Robbe-Grillet', in *Essais critiques*, 101–5.

Barthes, Roland (1984), 'La mort de l'auteur', in *Le Bruissement de la langue. Essais critiques IV*, Paris, Éditions du Seuil, 63–9.

Bolduc, Albert (March 1975), *Positif*.

Cahiers 95 (November 1995), 'Notes sur d'autres films'.

Chevassu, François (March 1967), *I and S*.

Cinéma 67 (March 1967).

Cinéma 74 (March 1974).

Cinéma 75 (April 1975).

Corpet, Olivier (ed.) (2001), *Alain Robbe-Grillet. Le Voyageur. Textes, causeries et entretiens 1947–2001*, Paris, Éditions Bourgois.

Deleuze, Gilles (1983), '"*Image Mouvement Image Temps*"': Cours Vincennes St-Denis: Bergson, propositions sur le cinéma', 18 May.

Doniol-Valcroze, Jacques (May 1963), 'Istanbul nous appartient', *Cahiers du cinéma*.

Fragola, Anthony N. and Smith, Roch C. (1992), *The Erotic Dream Machine: Interviews with Alain Robbe-Grillet on His Films*, Carbondale and Edwardsville, Southern Illinois University Press.

Gardies, André (2005), 'Le travail du double', in Prédal, *Robbe-Grillet Cinéaste*, 105–43.

Garsault, Alain (June 1974), *Positif*.

Grisolia, Michel (summer 1970), *Positif*.

Higgins, Lynn A., *New Novel, New Wave, New Politics: Fiction and the Representation of History in Post-war France*, Lincoln and London, University of Nebraska Press, 1996.

Kaiser, Grant E. (1974), 'L'amour et l'esthétique: "L'année dernière à Marienbad"', *South Atlantic Bulletin*, 39(4) (November): 113–20.

Lagier, Luc (2004), 'Dans le labyrinthe de Marienbad', StudioCanal Vidéo.

Leenhardt, Jacques (1973), *Lecture politique du roman:* La Jalousie *d'Alain Robbe-Grillet*, Paris, Éditions de Minuit.

Phillips, John (1999), *Forbidden Fictions: Pornography and Censorship in Twentieth-century French Literature*, London, Pluto Press.

Prédal, René (2005), 'Une œuvre gênante aux marges de la critique', in *Robbe-Grillet Cinéaste*, Études publiées sous la direction de René Prédal, Caen, Presses universitaires de Caen, 91–104.

Ricardou, Jean (1971), 'La fiction flamboyante', in *Pour une théorie du nouveau roman*, Paris, Éditions du Seuil.

Robbe-Grillet, Alain (1961), *L'Année dernière à Marienbad*, Paris, Éditions de Minuit.

Robbe-Grillet, Alain (1963a), 'Une voie pour le roman futur', in *Pour un nouveau roman*, Paris, Éditions de Minuit, 15–23.

Robbe-Grillet, Alain (1963b), 'Joë Bousquet le rêveur', in *Pour un nouveau roman*, 82–94.

Robbe-Grillet, Alain (1963c), 'Temps et description dans le récit d'aujourd'hui', in *Pour un nouveau roman*, 123–34.

Robbe-Grillet, Alain (1963d), *L'Immortelle*, Paris, Éditions de Minuit.

Robbe-Grillet, Alain (1974), *Glissements progressifs du plaisir*, Paris, Éditions de Minuit.

Robbe-Grillet, Alain (1987), *Angélique, ou l'enchantement*, Paris, Éditions de Minuit.

Robbe-Grillet, Alain (2002), *C'est Gradiva qui vous appelle*, Paris, Éditions de Minuit.

Robbe-Grillet, Alain (2005a), *Préface à une vie d'écrivain*, Paris, France Culture, Éditions du Seuil.

Robbe-Grillet, Alain (2005b), *Scénarios en rose et noir 1966–1983*, Textes et Photos réunis et présentés par Olivier Corpet and Emmanuelle Lambert, Paris, Librairie Arthème Fayard.

Waters, Julia (2000), *Intersexual Rivalry: A Reading in Pairs of Marguerite Duras and Alain Robbe-Grillet*, vol. 2, Bern and Oxford, Peter Lang.

Žižek, Slavoj (2002), *Welcome to the Desert of the Real! Five Essays on September 11 and Related Dates*, London, Verso.

1

The birth of a film-maker:
L'Année Dernière à Marienbad

It is one of the aims of this study to bring Robbe-Grillet's films to the attention of a wider public. For the reasons outlined in the Introduction, most of the films that bear his name as director are virtually unknown outside a very small coterie of intellectuals and academics. The single exception is *L'année dernière à Marienbad* which was the product of a collaboration between Robbe-Grillet as script-writer and Alain Resnais as director. This film has an enduring and iconic reputation as a leading example of experimental film-making, a reputation that is partly due to the award of the Lion d'Or for best film at the Venice Film Festival of 1961. The distributors had at first proved reluctant to release the film which they considered uncommercial, but thanks to this award, and to a number of private screenings for influential people, organised by the two Alains, it was distributed in France and Italy where it achieved a cult success.[1]

Marienbad was a new milestone in French, if not in world cinema. Along with other young European film-makers at the end of the 1950s and beginning of the 1960s – Godard, Chabrol, Truffaut, Bergman, Antonioni *et al.* – Resnais had begun to experiment with every aspect of the cinema apparatus, exploring new approaches to plot, character, sound track and use of camera, stressing improvisation and a freer *mise-en-scène* in external locations away from the artifice of the studio sets, and rejecting psychological realism. The young François Truffaut (22 years old) had begun this trend, to be dubbed the '*nouvelle vague*' or 'new wave', in a famous article entitled 'Une certaine tendance du

---

1 These included Sartre, Cocteau, Antonioni and André Breton to whom the film was originally going to be dedicated.

cinéma français' which appeared in the influential *Cahiers du cinéma* (no. 31) in January 1954. In this short piece, Truffaut had launched a scathing attack on what was known as the 'cinéma de qualité', an ossified coterie of established practitioners founded on the star system and, above all, on the adaptation of literary classics for the screen by a small number of scriptwriters and directors. Rejecting the latter's pursuit of psychological realism in canonical works of literature, Truffaut wanted cinema to create a language, an 'écriture' of its own instead of simply aping the literary, shifting the emphasis from writer to director, and thus initiating what was ironically termed a 'cinéma d'auteurs' or 'authors' cinema'.[2]

Auteurs

If *Marienbad* is an example of both the 'cinéma d'auteurs' and of the new wave, who was its author? The question of the film's paternity has not always proved a contentious one among critics. Generally speaking, and it must be said, according to the accepted convention of the cinema genre, *Marienbad* has tended to be attributed to Resnais as director. Yet this was not the case at the outset, and it is instructive to examine why the change in attribution occurred. *Les Cahiers du cinéma* (no. 123, September, 1961) published a long interview on the film's release with Jacques Rivette and André S. Labarthe which, exceptionally for the time, included Robbe-Grillet in addition to Resnais as director (see Prédal 2005: 92). The interview emphasised the role of Robbe-Grillet, as did the two critical reviews that followed by Labarthe and François Weyergans. Both articles speak of the film of Resnais *and* Robbe-Grillet. Moreover, in the interview, Resnais and Robbe-Grillet present a united front, in the manner of Joël and Ethan Coen.[3] *Image et Son* also credits both, as does *Positif* in which Raymond Borde accuses Resnais (and not Robbe-Grillet!) of making too literary a film![4] As Lynn A. Higgins points out, however, the entire new wave conceived itself in literary terms (and ironically so, given

---

2 For more on the *nouvelle vague*, see Hayward 1993: 232–9.

3 'Dans le dédale', by François Weyergans (1961), and '*Marienbad* année zéro', by André S. Labarthe (1968). An interview that included both men with Pierre Billard was also published in *Cinéma 61*, December 1961.

4 Raymond Borde, 'Attention littérature', *Positif*, no. 44, March 1962.

its rejection of the adaptation of the classics). New wave directors were authors who regarded the camera as their 'pen', suggesting an abiding 'literary frame of reference', and so in this respect, Robbe-Grillet is certainly no exception. (see Higgins 1996:10)

The majority of critics, then, attributed the success of the film as much to Robbe-Grillet as to Resnais, regarding both as belonging to this innovative new artistic movement. Yet, as Prédal suggests, Robbe-Grillet's debut in film contributed to the reopening of the fierce debate concerning film authorship which had only just died down (Prédal 2005: 92). It is, therefore, perhaps not entirely surprising that most later critics, many of whom are not familiar with Robbe-Grillet's work as a novelist, have unquestioningly attributed the film to Resnais alone. Even critics like Emma Wilson who are familiar with the context of the film's genesis and appreciative of Robbe-Grillet's artistic importance continue to speak of *Marienbad* as Resnais's film (see Wilson 2005; see also Wilson 2006: 67–86). This is also in part to be explained by the fact that the French film establishment's willingness to acknowledge Robbe-Grillet's contribution changed radically after the release of *L'Immortelle* which failed to meet with the approval of the two film journals, able to make or break reputations in 1960s France: *Les Cahiers du cinéma* and *Positif* (see Prédal 2005: 93). Alain Resnais's reputation as one of the leading exponents of new wave cinema also helps to explain the gradual focus on him as sole author of the film.

Emma Wilson's excellent study of *Marienbad* sensitively analyses the film as a fantasy constructed by two people in the present, rather than the memory of a past event, as in *Hiroshima mon amour*, and thus underscores the ways in which the film is set outside historical and political contexts.[5] The entire film, Robbe-Grillet tells us (Robbe-Grillet 1961: 12), is the 'story of a persuasion'. Character X (Giorgio Albertazzi) attempts to persuade character A (Delphine Seyrig) that they met one year earlier in the chateau where they are both staying or perhaps elsewhere, and that something passed between them at that time. While initially denying X's claim, A appears increasingly confused as the narrative progresses, a confusion to which X himself is not entirely immune, as we shall see presently. Nevertheless, it is the act of persuasion itself that is mis en scène in the film, as opposed

---

5 This is also the author's reading of the film's temporal aspects: see Chapter 2.

to the events in question, although this act is itself an event, and one also taking place in the imagination of the spectator. As Robbe-Grillet himself puts it, *Marienbad* 'is not a subsequent account of a love story which happened earlier; it is a story in the process of happening. This story is really in the process of being invented in your head and imagination.' (see Robbe-Grillet 1966: 88, quoted by Dittmar 1980: 238, n. 24)

This act of persuasion ironically also informs the critical debate surrounding the film's authorship. With regard to the latter, I must persuade you, my reader, of a number of things: of the plausibility of my interpretations, of the value and importance of Robbe-Grillet's films, and in relation to both of these, that *Marienbad* is as much Robbe-Grillet's as Resnais's work. The mainstay of my case will be that this is essentially an 'auteur' film in the literal sense of the word. While technically and artistically, *Marienbad* is very much a new wave film – in its use of camera, its privileging of external shots, and its innovative approach to character and plot, discarding psychological realism, as we shall see – the film has its roots in the era of the script-writer in France which the new wave was in the process of killing off. I shall also argue that the film contains the germs of all of Robbe-Grillet's main ideas and preoccupations, and as such offers a template for the reading of the films to come.

The issue of who owns the sexual fantasy that is the pretext for the entire film narrative remains uncertain, but is clearly one that will equally determine critical responses at the level of sexual politics: his fantasy, as the above scenario implies, and the sexual aggression of men towards women is on trial; hers, a hypothesis supported by his denial of their past – 'Non ... Non ... Je ne me souviens plus...Je ne me souviens plus moi-même'[6] (Robbe-Grillet 1961: 140), 'Non, non, non! ... C'est faux! [...] Ce n'était pas de force'[7] (ibid.: 157) – and the risk may be one of male film-makers depicting women as sexually promiscuous, as much a male stereotyping of women as their depiction as sexual innocents.

The more astute critics have hedged their bets, allocating the fantasy, if fantasy it is, to both. According to this view, X and A thus construct a past or virtual future together, a more subtle reading that allows for a fascinating exploration of the very nature of male/female

6 'No...No...I don't remember any more...I don't remember myself'
7 'No, no, no!...That's wrong!...[...] I didn't force you'

relationships. Resnais himself encouraged this interpretation on the film's release: 'on ne sait jamais si les images sont dans la tête de l'homme ou dans la tête de la femme. Il y a tout le temps un balance-ment entre les deux'[8] (Wilson 2006: 76). Moreover, a reading of the entire situation as dreamt or fantasised allows the spectator greater freedom to engage in the construction of meaning, and in particular, to identify with one or other protagonist.

A less positive view of male sexuality is implicit in the analogy between the X/A dialogue and a session of Freudian analysis. Such an analogy may suggest a number of related scenarios: false memory syndrome, A's amnesia following an accident, in which case the chateau may be a sanatorium rather than a hotel, with the other guests as inmates. Are we living in the dream (or fantasy, or nightmare) of A, the mental patient? The entire place is, after all, dreamlike, its archi-tecture in *trompe-l'œil* suggestive of an unreality associated in art with the surrealists whose influence on Robbe-Grillet was noted in the Introduction. In this reading, the situation assumes a linguistic as well as a sensory or experiential character in X's repeated addresses to A: 'Un soir, je suis monté jusqu'à votre chambre.'; 'Un soir, je suis monté jusqu'à votre chambre. Vous étiez seule.'; 'Une fois de plus'[9] (Robbe-Grillet 1961: 93, 102, 164). X's incantatory repetition of last year's events to A have a performative effect, as if creating a reality through words as in an act of hypnosis. In this reading, X constructs an entire sexual episode around the attempt to persuade A of their previous liaison. As in the analytical process, A (Analysand) begins to remember, as the relationship with X (as Analyst) progresses. The latter's imperative, 'Souvenez-vous' ('Remember') (ibid.: 69) then takes on a bullying and abusive tenor. We are irresistibly reminded here of feminist critiques of Freud's own manipulation of his female patients.[10] We have seen that, for Robbe-Grillet, the entire film is the story of a persuasion, 'une réalité que le héros crée par sa propre vision, par sa propre parole'[11] (Robbe-Grillet 1961: 12). All of this under-lines the linguistic nature of their relationship, and is not incompat-

8 'one never knows whether the images are in the man's or the woman's head. There is a constant movement from one to the other'
9 'One evening, I went up to your room.'; 'One evening, I went up to your room. You were alone.'; 'Once more'
10 See, for example, Cixous 1976.
11 'a reality that the hero creates through his own eyes, through his own speech'

ible with the transference that sometimes occurs between analyst and analysand, and that may also help to explain and define the sexual currents between them, where X is seen as paternally dominant over A's childlike submissiveness.

This linguistic performativity structures the whole film dialogue. As Wilson points out, words precede images, 'as if the extraordinarily tactile, sentient world of *Marienbad* [...] is called up, imagined as a result of the words we hear narrated' (Wilson 2006: 69). The images of the 'rape' scene are thus similarly brought into being by X's speech. As in fairy-tales, it is as if things happen by magic when the right words are pronounced: X's invocation, 'je pénètre à nouveau dans votre chambre' immediately produces shots of A's room.[12] The performative power of speech is thus brought visually to life, and in Lacanian terms, the very authority of the 'Name of the Father', as inhering in language as the medium of the male symbolic realm, is asserted. In addition to its central role in the relationship between film and spectator, and film and critic, and its replication at a number of levels within the filmic text, the act of persuasion is also an equally fitting description of the extratextual or paratextual relationship between the two auteurs.

T. Jefferson Kline has argued that in describing the story as 'essentially the record of a communication between two people [...] one of them putting suggestions and the other resisting, until they end in agreement', Robbe-Grillet was unconsciously describing his relationship with Resnais (see Kline 2006: 212). Robbe-Grillet has repeatedly claimed that Resnais and he saw eye to eye in almost every respect. However, there were a few differences of opinion before shooting began which carried over into the making of the film from which Robbe-Grillet was absent.[13] For instance, while Robbe-Grillet wanted a theatre actress for the main female role, Delphine Seyrig was Resnais's choice (see Lagier 2004). A comparison of Robbe-Grillet's script, as published in the *cinéroman* and the film shot by Resnais does also reveal three main differences of note. Robbe-Grillet had wanted the film to be shot in the spas of Salso Maggiore near Parma, or at the casino in Vichy, but Resnais opted to shoot in three chateaux near Munich: Nymphenburg, Amalienburg, and Schleissheim, and

12 'I enter your room once again'
13 Robbe-Grillet was not present during any of the shooting, having left for Istanbul to start work on *L'Immortelle* immediately after completing the *Marienbad* script.

at the Munich Antiquarium, with interiors shot in the Photosonor studios in Paris (Robbe-Grillet 2005: 204; Wilson 2006: 68). Resnais did however preserve the fundamental contrast envisaged by Robbe-Grillet between the interior and exterior spaces, the former defined in terms of baroque circles and spirals, exemplified by the staircase and stucco ornaments, the latter a park designed with classical precision, defined by squares and rectangles. Reversing the dichotomy of the interior and exterior spaces of *La Jalousie*, Robbe-Grillet's script locates disorder and confusion inside rather than outside, a pattern reflecting the internal disorder of A's (and perhaps also X's) mental state. These effects are accompanied and heightened inside the chateau by a strong sense of claustrophobia, which is reflected to some degree by the labyrinthine outside spaces. For Grant E. Kaiser, this effect is linked to what he calls the 'prison of love'. Most scenes, he notes, take place inside the chateau, in which doors and windows are rarely in view, so that the spectator's gaze is constantly directed towards the interior, an effect reinforced by the omnipresent mirrors (see Kaiser 1974: 117–18).

The second difference constitutes a more radical change. Robbe-Grillet had envisaged a realistic and brutal act of rape of A by X:

> Assez rapide et brutale scène de viol. A est basculée en arrière, X lui maintenant les poignets (d'une seule main) sous la taille. A se débat, mais sans résultat aucun. Elle ouvre la bouche comme pour crier; mais X, penché sur elle, introduit aussitôt dans cette bouche, en guise de bâillon, une menue pièce de lingerie fine qu'il tenait dans l'autre main [...] Cheveux étalés de la victime et son costume en désordre.[14] (Robbe-Grillet 1961: 156–7)

This crude scenario of sexual force which is recognisably a product of Robbe-Grillet's sexual fantasies is metaphoricised by Resnais, as the camera rather than X penetrates A's room, and the scene becomes white, implying a violent act. This change might be interpreted as censorship on Resnais' part, but it is arguably more subtle, more artistically effective, and perhaps more in keeping with the 'dream' hypothesis than the more explicit scenario intended by Robbe-Grillet.

---

14 'Fairly rapid and brutal rape scene. A is thrown back with X gripping her wrists (with one hand) beneath her waist. A struggles but in vain. She opens her mouth as if to scream, but X, bending over her, immediately stuffs a small piece of fine lingerie which he was holding in his other hand into her mouth to gag her [...] the victim's hair is dishevelled and her clothes in disorder.'

Resnais's rewriting of the rape scene also makes possible a more sympathetic view of X, thus facilitating a cathartic response on the part of spectators of either sex.

More serious, even, than the censorship of a sexually explicit scene is the third major departure from Robbe-Grillet's script, the scale of which might be considered to have a significant artistic impact. The baroque organ music employed by Resnais seems incompatible with a narrative that intentionally eschews harmony, coherence and historical specificity. Organ music, for Robbe-Grillet, was a type of church music that suggests too harmonious an atmosphere, whereas he had himself planned to use a music constructed around noises – a 'musique concrète' as it was called in the 1960s, and one pregnant with meaning. This music would have had a jarring effect that would have more effectively complemented the film's verbal and visual incoherence:

> J'avais écrit au contraire une musique faite pour crisper. Au lieu de cette belle continuité enveloppante de l'orgue, je voulais une structure de trous et de chocs [...] J'avais imaginé une composition à partir des bruits essentiellement réalistes qu'on entend dans un hôtel à l'ancienne mode comme celui-là. Par exemple les portes d'ascenseur, ces portes métalliques en tiges articulées qui font un très beau bruit [...] ou bien les sonneries des différents appels: du portier, de la femme de chambre, etc., [...] Cette musique, au sens où j'entends le mot musique pour un film, aurait certes eu un effet totalement différent sur le spectateur.[15] (Robbe-Grillet 1970: 133–4)

In the main, however, the rest of Robbe-Grillet's script is faithfully followed by Resnais and so it does not seem unreasonable to argue that, as author of the screenplay and shooting-script, Robbe-Grillet played at least as important a role in the creation of the film. Robbe-Grillet points out that the French word, 'réalisateur' suggests someone who converts a virtuality into a real image on the screen (Fragola and Smith 1992: 26). In this sense, to employ an analogy of which the

---

15 'I had written music designed to set the nerves on edge. Instead of this all-enveloping organ music, I had envisaged a structure full of holes and shocks [...] I had imagined a score based on realistic noises such as one hears in old-style hotels like the one in the film. For example, lift doors, those metal doors with gates that make a very beautiful noise [...] or else the bells that summon the various employees – porters, chamber-maids, etc., [...] That kind of music, in the sense I conceive the word music for a film, would certainly have had quite a different impact on the spectator.'

latter would have approved, Robbe-Grillet is the architect and Resnais the builder.

Most persuasive of all the arguments in favour of a Robbe-Grillet authorship is perhaps the fact that the film narrative is obsessively focussed on objects and characteristics associated with Robbe-Grillet's sexual proclivities (and this, despite his much-vaunted scientific attention to the surface of things).[16]

The uncanny

As noted earlier, the man, X's initial approach to the woman, A rests upon an insistence on her familiarity: 'Vous êtes toujours la même. J'ai l'impression de vous avoir quittée hier'[17] (Robbe-Grillet 1961: 46); 'Vous êtes toujours aussi belle'[18] (ibid.: 48). On the other hand, this feeling is countered by the woman's distance. Her subsequent denials of any previous history between the couple create an opposition between the familiar and the strange that runs throughout the film, and that is reflected in its many dreamlike elements. A disturbing and at times threatening atmosphere is generated by the other guests' static quality, reminiscent of dolls, marionettes or statues, while a statue in the grounds of the chateau appears in one key scene to come alive: 'la statue sur son socle, elle, à cause de sa situation, paraît au contraire grandir par rapport à eux'[19] (ibid.: 139). The characters interpret this statue variously as representing an historical relationship (Charles III and his wife) (ibid.: 76), a mythical relationship (Andromache and Pyrrhus) (ibid.: 71), and the story of their own passion, signposted by a number of pregnant references (for example, 'Vue de la statue du couple déjà décrite et montrée plusieurs fois dans le film')[20] (ibid.: 128). As Kaiser observes, a broken statue is visible as the narrative moves towards its climax (ibid.: 158; see Kaiser 1974:

16 Dittmar makes this point, claiming with some justification that this disjunction 'inspires and shapes his work' (1980: 218–19). The tension between the formalistic and the sexual will be further explored in Chapter 5.

17 'You're always the same. I feel as if we parted only yesterday.'

18 'You are still just as beautiful.'

19 'because of its position, the statue on its socle appears to get bigger compared to them.'

20 'View of the statue of the couple already described and shown several times in the film.'

119). Resnais himself remarked that the film could be described as 'a documentary about a statue' (see Labarthe and Rivette 1961: 3). The statue's apparent animation and many other oneiric aspects have helped to reinforce the view, noted earlier, that the entire narrative is dreamt by X or by A. This dream hypothesis resonates closely with the uncanny atmosphere and labyrinthine setting of the hotel and grounds, a 'dédale où on peut se perdre' being a metaphor for the whole story.[21]

These elements have a strongly Freudian resonance. In his essay, 'The Uncanny' (Freud 1985 [1919]), Freud attempts to capture the feeling of 'worrying strangeness' that is linguistically embedded in the German word, 'unheimlich'. The feeling of strangeness that we sometimes experience is not the opposite, Freud argues, but paradoxically the *expression* of intimacy, a point underlined by his philological unearthing of the word 'unheimlich' as originally an extension, rather than a simple negation, of the 'heimlich' (homely or familiar). What frightens us most is sometimes a familiar scene or object that has been repressed and that some event brings back to the surface. The word 'unheimlich', then, has a semantic instability that captures that feeling of ambivalence we sometimes experience in both our waking and dream states, that something we are encountering is at the same time familiar and agreeable. Freud illustrates this feeling with reference to dolls or waxwork figures, as represented in a story, 'The Sandman', by E. T. A. Hoffman. This tale also plays upon an uncertainty as to whether an object is living or inanimate, which can be identified in the movement of the extras reminiscent of chess pieces, especially in the park scenes, and above all, in the repeated focus on the statue which at times, as we have seen, appears to come alive, upon the double and repetition, and the associated sense of the uncanny. Other aspects of the film create this uncanny effect when the distinction between imagination and reality is effaced. The uncanny is also connected with magic and sorcery and the return of the dead, both of which are suggested by a situation in which a man wishes to resurrect events through an incantatory use of language.[22] Not least, finally, the uncanny effect is created by the erosion of a stable identity for A who may have a number of different personae, as metaphori-

---

21 'a maze in which you can get lost'
22 The uncanny is also discussed in the context of *L'Immortelle* in Chapter 4. On images of the 'undead', see Chapter 6.

cally suggested by the discovery by X of many different photos of her in the drawer in her bedroom.

Marienbad as *Urtext*

As the first instance of Robbe-Grillet's cinematic œuvre, *Marienbad* contains the seeds of all his later work for the cinema, and as such, heralds a cinematic corpus that has its roots in the new wave, while deviating from it in a number of important respects. These themes and forms fall broadly into four principal though inevitably overlapping categories: the artistic, the ideological and the philosophical, the erotic, and the temporal.

Artistic

Musical forms complement (or rather, function in counterpoint to) the visual in *Marienbad*. Like a work of musical composition, *Marienbad* is made up of patterns repeated like leitmotifs. Dittmar describes our experience of the film as a whole as 'polyphonic', arguing that meaning depends on the interlacing of repetitions, juxtapositions and variations (1980: 233). This structure, akin to musical leitmotifs, according to which a particular element such as the Nim game generates an entire thematic pattern (in this case, game-playing as characterising the relationship between X and A), is one that will be repeated from film to film. The Nim game, played by other 'guests' in the chateau and which it is possible to lose and win at the same time is also an example of the ludic elements of all Robbe-Grillet's films (ibid.: 220, 227). We saw earlier that extras who move slowly through the grounds of the chateau resemble pieces on a game board, an effect enhanced by lines of pyramid-shaped bushes framing the park.[23] The doubts and ambiguities *mis en scène* in *Marienbad*, which are visually troped by its labyrinths, also form part of this ludic dimension, as does the self-reflexivity of the stage play that opens the film, a *mise en abyme* of the creation of both fantasy and the work of fiction.

Robbe-Grillet's filmic imagination is primarily a visual one, and all of his later films will be seen to place great importance on this visual dimension, often under the influence of surrealist painters

23 See Chapter 2 on music in the films, and Chapter 3 on games.

such as Magritte.[24] Though shot in black and white, *Marienbad* is an intensely visual work, the sweeping vistas of the park contrasting with the claustrophobic interiors of the chateau, and while the make-up and costumes of the actors were obviously Resnais's responsibility as director, these visual aspects are in perfect harmony with Robbe-Grillet's approach to film. He refused to write a script for Antonioni, for example, because the latter considered their respective roles to be utterly discrete:

> Mais quand je lui ai parlé concrètement du film qu'on allait faire, et que je lui ai dit: «Au début, on voit sur l'écran...», Antonioni m'a immédiatement arrêté. Il m'a dit: «Ecoute, non! Tu me racontes une histoire, et moi je te dis ce qu'on voit sur l'écran. » Je lui ai répondu: «Si je pense à un film, je ne pense pas à une histoire, je pense à ce qu'on voit sur l'écran, et je ne peux te parler que de cela! Si tu tiens à une histoire, prends un de mes romans et fais-en un film.»[25] (Robbe-Grillet 2005: 202)

All these visual elements are anchored in the subjectivity of the two main characters, and as such are consistent with the new novel's approach to fiction. *Marienbad* is, above all, a *nouveau roman* transferred onto the screen, and as such, conforms to all of the genre's prescriptions for the representation of an inner rather than an outer reality, as well as to its prioritisation of form over content. Indeed, the film bears close similarities in these respects to Robbe-Grillet's best-known novel, *La Jalousie*, published just four years earlier. As in the novel, *Marienbad*'s female protagonist is named A (the most open vowel in the French language, suggestive of a sexual receptivity), while the two men, X and M, also unconventionally named by letters,

24 This concern with the visual dimension was clearly shared by Resnais in his concern with costume. Wilson tells us that the leading actress, Delphine Seyrig as A was dressed by Chanel: 'In these chiaroscuro garments, each perfectly tailored, sculpting Seyrig's body, veiling yet revealing its shape, she is a fashion icon (Brigitte Bardot later asked Chanel to dress her in the style of *Marienbad*)' (2006: 73). She compares her eyelashes to 'dark flowers or insects', and the androgynous sensuality of her hair to a Lee Miller or Man Ray image (ibid.). See Chapter 2 for a more detailed discussion of the visual and audial aspects.

25 'But when I spoke to him in detail about the film we were going to make, saying "First, we'll see on the screen...", Antonioni immediately stopped me, saying "No! Listen, you tell me a story, and I tell you what we see on the screen." My response to him was "If I think about a film, I don't think about a story, I think about what is seen on the screen, and that's all I can speak about! If you want a story, take one of my novels and make a film of it."'

mirror the two male figures of the novel who similarly lack the full names customary in realist fiction: in *La Jalousie*, the husband has no name, and indeed remains a shadowy figure, little more than an implication of the text, and the lover is simply Franck. The narrative of the novel embraces an obsessively jealous male perspective, for which mundane details of behaviour, such as the positioning of arms on adjacent chairs, are viewed in the context of an assumed sexual affair. Similarly, as Kaiser puts it, camera, focalisation and voice-over in *Marienbad* are all directed by a 'loving look' (1974: 114; see also Lagier 2004). The many lacunae and contradictions in the text also echo those of *La Jalousie*, in which a sexual relationship between A and Franck may or may not have occurred.

Ideological and philosophical aspects

As an example of art that is very much for its own sake, as a narrative that eschews any fixed social or political message, the film is in part a reaction against the notion of commitment in literature and art propounded by an older generation of French intellectuals, notably, Jean-Paul Sartre, Simone de Beauvoir and Albert Camus. A minority of critics have attempted to read the film against the background of the Algerian war, in its closing stages when the film was being made (see, for instance, Burch 2005: 28), but there is little evidence of any overt or even covert historical references. Such readings, while ingenious, do not convey the film's specificity. In a Marxist perspective, any work inevitably bears the marks of the time and culture that produced it, but this is not the same thing as saying that it contains a clear and dominant historical and/or political resonance. It is more accurate to say that, in its lugubrious atmosphere, the film reflects the cold-war climate of its time, though without any express pedagogical intentions. These gloomy undercurrents may have unconsciously influenced Resnais's choice of location. Marienbad, a famous Czech spa, was the site of Goethe's marriage proposal, the event that inspired his romantic elegy of emotional pain and grief, *Die Leiden des Jungen Werthers* (Kline 2006: 208). According to Kline, this literary intertext is paralleled by a real event. In 1936, the psychoanalyst, Jacques Lacan gave a paper on the mirror stage at Marienbad (ibid.: 209). However, there is a more interesting, and in my view, more apposite connection: Lacan's theory of the mirror stage is essentially a moment of loss and of the foundation of lifelong lack, a moment when the young child becomes aware of its complete separateness from the mother. Absence and loss are dominant emotions in a film centring on the situation of a woman without memory of a past or plans for the future. It is as if A, victim of an unknown traumatic event (perhaps a rape that needs to be therapeutically exorcised) were a suitable case for analysis – a situation which, as we have seen, is one among a number of possible readings of *Marienbad*.

Eroticism

After Resnais expunged the graphic rape scene, *Marienbad* was left without any explicit erotic content. Nevertheless, the film retains in embryo all of those themes and motifs for which Robbe-Grillet's later work will become notorious: an obsession with beautiful young women, male sexual aggression, the repeated representation of fetishistic objects (in this case, foot fetishism in the focus on A's broken shoes, which are in turn closely linked to broken glass and A's tinkling laughter, all castratory motifs), and the use of film noir as an erotically charged vehicle.[26] As others have averred, such elements militate against Robbe-Grillet's claim to represent the truth of our internal reality with a scientific objectivity. Early critics, such as Doris McGinty Davis, under the spell of the author's theoretical pronouncements, are thus drawn to conclude that it is impossible to know Robbe-Grillet through his work (1965: 483).[27] In the same article, however, and in apparent self-contradiction, McGinty Davis notes that, in *Le Voyeur* (1955), the circle and the figure of 8 suggest the theme of strangulation (of a very young girl, we remember) (ibid.: 481). The author's own erotic penchant for young girls may not have been widely known in the 1960s, but it would seem difficult to argue that such a theme

26 Wilson sees the white feathers of A's peignoir as a fetish because 'commemorative' of living birds (2005: 26).

27 Compare this early reading of Robbe-Grillet with the more nuanced approach of later critics who tend to emphasise the amenability of the work to readings that argue for a more subjective character: for example, Dittmar, for whom 'Rather, it is an obsessive effort to distort or avoid facts, springing from a well of unarticulated passions' (1980: 218); and Wilson, for whom A and X share the same sexual fantasy (2006: 85) – as we saw earlier, a politically more acceptable view than that of an implied seduction or rape – suggesting that this fantasy may have its origins in an authorial subjectivity, whether conscious or unconscious.

would form part of a scientifically objective view of the world. In any case, one cannot help but think that Robbe-Grillet's insistence on scientific objectivity at the time – he considerably modified this position later – was designed to mask the undercurrents of perversion that run through all his work.[28]

Time in *Marienbad*

In film, Robbe-Grillet wrote in 1963, there is only one grammatical mode, the present indicative: 'Film et roman se rencontrent en tout cas, aujourd'hui, dans la construction d'instants, d'intervalles et de successions qui n'ont plus rien à voir avec ceux des horloges ou du calendrier'[29] (1963: 130); 'What interests me are the possibilities of putting on the same level the past, the present, the future, the imaginary, etc. [...] Any other process that tries to re-establish temporality is a process that reveals a nostalgia for literature, since literature possesses the entire range of grammatical tenses' (Fragola and Smith 1992: 149–50).

Gilles Deleuze archly observes, however, that the present tense is not a simple dimension. Adopting St Augustine's fine formulation, he speaks of 'a present of the future, a present of the present and a present of the past' (1989: 100). With this complexity of the present perhaps in mind, Robbe-Grillet argues that time has been perceived as the main character of cinema as of the novel, since 'toute œuvre cinématographique moderne serait une réflexion sur la mémoire humaine, ses incertitudes, son entêtement, ses drames, etc'[30] (1963: 130). Deleuze notes that, in the case of *Marienbad*, the author's and the director's conceptions of time were fundamentally different. Robbe-Grillet criticised Resnais for being too interested in memory and forgetting. While Robbe-Grillet's focus was the present, Resnais saw the characters as inhabiting different versions of the past:

> Resnais conceived *Last Year*... like his other films, in the form of sheets or regions of past, while Robbe-Grillet sees time in the form of points

28 See Chapters 5 and 6 for a detailed exploration of the erotic elements.

29 'The cinema and the novel come together nowadays in the construction of moments, of intervals and links that have nothing to do with those of the clock or the calendar.'

30 'all films are reflections on human memory and its uncertainties, its insistence, its dramas, etc.'

of present. If *Last Year*...could be divided, the man X might be said to be closer to Resnais, and the woman A closer to Robbe-Grillet. The man basically tries to envelop the woman with continuous sheets of which the present is the narrowest, like the advance of a wave, whilst the woman, at times wary, at times stiff, at times almost convinced, jumps from one bloc to another, continually crossing an abyss between two points, two simultaneous presents. In any event, the two authors [...] are no longer in the domain of the real and the imaginary but in time, in the even more alarming domain of the true and the false. Of course the real and the imaginary continue their circuit, but only as the base of a higher figure. This is no longer, or no longer only, the *indiscernible becoming* of distinct images; it is *undecidable alternatives* between circles of past, *inextricable differences* between peaks of present. With Resnais and Robbe-Grillet, an understanding occurs, all the stronger for being based on two opposed conceptions of time which crashed into each other. The coexistence of sheets of virtual past, and the simultaneity of peaks of de-actualized present, are the two direct signs of time itself. (Deleuze 1989: 104–5)

For Robbe-Grillet, it is misleading to dwell on the adjective 'last' in the film title, because there is no more a 'last year' than there is a lost love, his characters inhabiting a present without past or future.

Presents and the incomposible

Deleuze goes much further in his theorising about the narrative's 'undecidable alternatives', coining the term, 'incompossible' to denote the idea of a number of different presents in Robbe-Grillet's cinema that are simultaneously possible and yet impossible. We note that Deleuze's reading is in tune with Robbe-Grillet's own emphasis on post-Einsteinian physics as the basis of his thinking about time:

Thus narration will consist of the distribution of different presents to different characters, so that each forms a combination that is plausible and possible in itself, but where all of them together are 'incompossible', and where the inexplicable is thereby maintained and created. In *Last Year*... it is X who knew A (so A does not remember or is lying), and it is A who does not know X (so X is mistaken or playing a trick on her). Ultimately, the three characters correspond to the three different presents, but in such a way as to 'complicate' the inexplicable instead of throwing light on it; in such a way as to bring about its existence instead of suppressing it: what X lives in is a present of past, A lives in a present of future, so that the difference exudes or assumes a present of present (the third, the husband), all implicated in each other. The repetition distributes its variations on the three presents [...] this new mode of narration still remains human, even though it constitutes a lofty form of non-sense. It does not yet tell us the essential point. The essential point rather appears if we think of an earthly event which is assumed to be transmitted to different planets, one of which would receive it at the same time (at the speed of light), but the second more quickly, and the third less quickly, hence before it happened and after. The latter would not yet have received it, the second would already have received it, the first would be receiving it, in three simultaneous presents bound into the same universe. This would be a sidereal time, a system of relativity, where the characters would be not so much human as planetary, and the accents not so much subjective as astro-nomical, in a plurality of worlds constituting the universe [...] It would be a pluralist cosmology [...] where one and the same event is played out in these different worlds, in incompatible versions. (Ibid: 101–2)[31]

These theoretical differences, which mattered so much to the two Alains, may be insignificant for the spectator who perceives only opposing temporal points of view. Whether aspects of the present or of the past, the images in question are still shared. Once again, Deleuze is especially perceptive:

here the memory is for two characters. But it is a memory which is still shared, since it refers to the same givens, affirmed by one of them and refused or denied by the other. What happens is that the character X revolves in a circuit of past which includes A as shining point, as 'aspect', whilst A is in regions which do not include X or do so only in a nebulous way. Will A allow herself to be attracted into X's sheet, or will the latter be shattered and unhinged by A's resistances which are rolled up in her own sheets? (Ibid.: 117)

In *Marienbad*, the real problem is one of persuading the spectator not to read the temporal elements of film as before, not to interpret *L'Année dernière à Marienbad*, for instance, despite its title, in terms of

31 *La Belle captive* similarly aims to subvert narrative temporality, and offers further examples of Deleuze's 'incompossible'. For instance, in one scene, Marie-Ange is found in the living tableau, and in the same sequence, we suddenly find her also on the beach, after which there is a cut back to Walter, and so, as Anthony Fragola points out, there are at least three temporalities in play here: 'Walter would represent conventional time; Marie-Ange on the beach would represent atemporal time, a form of dream time; and the portrait would represent an inter-mediate time between the two, an idealization' (Fragola and Smith 1992: 105).

a conventional psychology of memory and forgetting, of recognition and denial. These questions, Robbe-Grillet bluntly maintains, have no meaning. Characteristically, his self-exegesis is considerably clearer than all others'. Only the present is important where it truly counts – in the mind of the spectator:

> L'univers dans lequel se déroule tout le film est [...] celui d'un présent perpétuel qui rend impossible tout recours à la mémoire. C'est un monde sans passé qui se suffit à lui-même à chaque instant et qui s'efface au fur et à mesure. Cet homme, cette femme commencent à exister seulement lorsqu'ils apparaissent sur l'écran pour la première fois; auparavant ils ne sont rien; et, une fois la projection terminée, ils ne sont plus rien de nouveau. Leur existence ne dure que ce que dure le film. Il ne peut y avoir de réalité en dehors des images que l'on voit, des paroles que l'on entend.[32] (Robbe-Grillet 1963: 131)

Thus, the story in *Marienbad* does not occupy two years or three days but exactly an hour and a half (ibid.). The love affair was not an event of the past or of the imagination, but was happening before our eyes in the hic et nunc, since (in the world of film) 'il n'y a pas plus d'*ailleurs* possible que d'*autrefois*'[33] (ibid.).

Robbe-Grillet admits that the temporal structure can only be subjective (ibid.: 132), and yet refers to the time imagined by the spectator as the only one that matters: 'de même que le seul temps qui importe est celui du film, le seul «personnage» important est le spectateur; c'est dans sa tête que se déroule toute l'histoire, qui est exactement imaginée par lui'[34] (ibid.). Furthermore, he adds, 'l'œuvre n'est pas un témoignage sur une réalité extérieure, mais elle est à elle-même sa propre réalité'[35] (ibid.).

32 'The world in which the entire film unfolds is [...] that of a perpetual present which makes any recourse to memory impossible. It is a world without a past which is self-sufficient at every single moment and which gradually effaces itself. This man and this woman begin to exist only when they appear on screen for the first time; before then, they are nothing, and once the projection of the film ends, they are nothing once again. Their existence only lasts for as long as the film lasts. There can be no reality outside the images one sees, the words one hears.'

33 'there is no possibility of an *elsewhere* or of a *previously*'

34 'in the same way that the only time that matters is the time of the film, the only "character" of importance is the spectator; the whole story is imagined by her and happens in her head'

35 'The work of art does not bear witness to an external reality, but is in itself its own reality.'

These different conceptions of time for author and director obviously have their roots in different philosophies of reality. Deleuze suggests that one major difference between Resnais and Robbe-Grillet in *Marienbad* relates to the real and the imaginary:

> for Resnais, there is always something real which persists, and notably spatio-temporal co-ordinates maintaining their reality, even though they come into conflict with the imaginary. It is in this way that Resnais maintains that something actually did happen 'Last Year...' [...] While in Robbe-Grillet everything happens 'in the head' of the characters, or, better, of the viewer himself. (1989: 103–4)

Based on the notion of different presents, Deleuze's analysis, which is closer to Robbe-Grillet's, is undoubtedly an ingenious one, helping the spectator to reconcile the disparities between X's and A's versions of events by viewing the film narrative as primarily rooted in modern conceptions of temporality. On the other hand, his readings are highly theoretical, and pose the question of whether Robbe-Grillet's cinema is to be understood on an intellectual level, or experienced viscerally or sensorially in the manner of much modern art. In this regard, and despite his self-avowed scientific training, the author's own view of time in the film as psychological and subjective is much more that of an artist than Resnais's.

As we shall see in Chapter 2, this achronological conception of temporality in large part determines Robbe-Grillet's privileging of the shot (rather than sequence) as a timeless dimension, and his revolutionary approach to sound and speech as frequently inhibiting any attempt on the spectator's part to construct a meaningful narrative chronology.

Such a plethora of possible readings is testimony to the film's artistic depth, one created, above all, by Robbe-Grillet as the work's principal imaginative source. Directors are notorious for making wholesale changes to shooting scripts, but in this case, as we have seen, Resnais actually made very few modifications, whether because he genuinely agreed with most of its contents, or in deference to an author he openly admired. Resnais was a young man, at the beginning of his long career in the cinema. Until *Hiroshima mon amour* which Resnais had just made with Marguerite Duras, he had only directed shorts, and was perhaps less confident about asserting his authority as a director of full-length films than he might have been at a later stage in his career. Moreover, both films had constraints attached to them: while the *Marienbad* project carried with it the constraint of a prewritten script, *Hiroshima*, it seems, was given to Resnais on the proviso that it be filmed in Japan and have the atomic bomb as its subject (Robbe-Grillet 2005: 198).

Whatever its paternity, *Marienbad* has had an enormous influence on later film-makers – Stanley Kubrick's *The Shining*, in which events and figures from the past haunt an isolated hotel in which reality and nightmare are increasingly confused, has often been cited as one among many examples (see, for instance, Lagier 2004) – and as a film of the *nouvelle vague* in every sense, *Marienbad* provided Robbe-Grillet himself with the artistic and professional springboard into a long career as filmmaker, during which he would build upon and, in a number of important respects, deviate from these 'new wave' beginnings.

By the time *Marienbad* was completed, Robbe-Grillet had already started shooting *L'Immortelle*, the first of ten films directed as well as written by him. However, as he would quickly discover, the control that he might reasonably expect to have of a film of which he was both author and director was still not quite within his grasp.

References

Billard, Pierre (1961), 'Entrevue avec Alain Resnais et Alain Robbe-Grillet', *Cinéma 61*, November–December.

Borde, Raymond (1962), 'Attention littérature', *Positif*, no. 44, March.

Burch, Noël (2005), 'Retour sur *L'Immortelle*', in Prédal, *Robbe-Grillet Cinéaste*, 25–33.

Cixous, Hélène (1976), *Portrait de Dora*, Paris, Éditions du Seuil des femmes.

Deleuze, Gilles (1989), *Cinema 2: The Time Image*, London, Athlone Press.

Dittmar, Linda (1980), 'Structures of Metaphor in Robbe-Grillet's *Last Year in Marienbad*', *Boundary 2: An International Journal of Literature and Culture*, 8(3): 215–39.

Fragola, Anthony N. and Smith, Roch C. (1992), *The Erotic Dream Machine: Interviews with Alain Robbe-Grillet on His Films*, Carbondale and Edwardsville, Southern Illinois University Press.

Freud, Sigmund (1985 [1919]), 'Das Unheimliche'; trans. 'The Uncanny', Harmondsworth, Middlesex, Pelican Freud Library 14: *Art and Literature*, Penguin Books, 335–76.

Hayward, Susan (1993), *French National Cinema*, London and New York, Routledge.

Higgins, Lynn A. (1996), *New Novel, New Wave, New Politics: Fiction and the Representation of History in Postwar France*, Lincoln and London, University of Nebraska Press.

Kaiser, Grant E. (Nov. 1974), 'L'amour et l'esthétique: "L'année Dernière A Marienbad"', *South Atlantic Bulletin*, 39(4): 113–20.

Kline, T. Jefferson (2006), 'Last Year at Marienbad: High Modern and Postmodern', in Fred Perry (ed.), *Masterpieces of Modern Cinema*, Bloomington, Indiana, Indiana University Press, 208–35.

Labarthe, André S. (1968), '*Marienbad* année zéro', in *Cahiers du cinéma*, no. 203, August.

Labarthe, André S. and Rivette, Jacques (September 1961), 'Entretien avec Resnais et Robbe-Grillet', *Cahiers du cinéma*, 21:123.

Lagier, Luc (2004), 'Dans le labyrinthe de Marienbad', réalisé par Luc Lagier, *L'Année dernière à Marienbad*, Studio Canal DVD.

McGinty Davis, Doris (1965), '"Le Voyeur" et "L'Année dernière à Marienbad"', *French Review*, 38(4): 477–84.

Prédal, René (2005), 'Une œuvre gênante aux marges de la critique', in *Robbe-Grillet Cinéaste*, Études publiées sous la direction de René Prédal, Caen, Presses universitaires de Caen, 91–104.

Robbe-Grillet, Alain (1961), *L'Année dernière à Marienbad*, Paris, Éditions de Minuit.

Robbe-Grillet, Alain (1963), 'Temps et Description dans le récit d'aujourd'hui', in *Pour un nouveau roman*, Paris, Éditions de Minuit, 123–34.

Robbe-Grillet, Alain (1966), 'Objectivity and Subjectivity', *New Hungarian Quarterly*, 22: 88.

Robbe-Grillet, Alain (1970), 'Le cinéma selon Alain Robbe-Grillet, Tapuscrit annoté d'Alain Robbe-Grillet, textes inédits; Annexe à l'article d'André Gardies, 'Le travail du double', in Prédal, *Robbe-Grillet Cinéaste*, 111–43.

Robbe-Grillet, Alain (2005), *Préface à une vie d'écrivain*, Paris, France Culture, Éditions du Seuil.

Weyergans, François (1961), 'Dans le dédale,' *Cahiers du cinéma*, 20(123): 22–7.

Wilson, Emma (2005), 'Material Relics: Resnais, Memory and the Senses', *French Studies*, 59(1): 25–30.

Wilson, Emma (2006), *Alain Resnais*, French Film Directors, Manchester, Manchester University Press.

2

Sight and sound:
harmony in counterpoint?

In statements and interviews with critics throughout his career, Robbe-Grillet has appeared to privilege the visual medium, declaring a preference for the silent era: 'silent film [...] is more interesting for me, since sound film has been taken over by dialogue [...] sound film suddenly produced an enormous effect of regression, announced by Eisenstein in his famous "Statement on the Future of Sound Film"' (Fragola and Smith 1992: 148, 161) In this regard, Robbe-Grillet's cinematic world echoes Antonin Artaud's notion that the stage must reflect the internal life of the spectator. Artaud suggested that language had become devoid of meaning, and only a new visual language would reveal the inner drama of the spectator (1964: 190).

On the other hand, despite its apparent opposition to sound in film, Eisenstein's 'Statement' did suggest that this innovation could have artistic advantages, and although he initially appeared to find sound artistically unchallenging, Robbe-Grillet admits to a strong interest in film soundtracks and the possibilities that these offer for experimental approaches. He argued in his early theoretical essays that writers are drawn to work in film precisely because it is a medium that combines both dimensions, and moreover, 'non pas tant l'image que la bande sonore – le son des voix, les bruits, les ambiances, les musiques – et surtout la possibilité d'agir sur deux sens à la fois, l'œil et l'oreille'[1] (1963: 128). Indeed, he innovates enthusiastically at the audial level, using music and sound effects in strikingly original ways,

---

1 'not merely the image but the sound track – the sound of voices, noises, les ambiances, music – and above all, the ability to act on two senses at once, the eye and the ear'

exploring the artistic advantages of pitting sound and image against each other, rather than seeking to harmonise them as in more traditional cinema. I shall examine first his approach to the visual medium of film and how he works creatively at this level.

The visual

Like the film-makers of the *nouvelle vague*, Robbe-Grillet may be considered an 'auteur' in every sense of this term, but especially, perhaps, in his use of the camera, which like the writer's pen, is the director's instrument. Robbe-Grillet's experimental approach to camera use and the visual dimension has created some of cinema's most memorable imagery: Violette's dance around the fire in *L'Eden et après*, the self-consciously parodic dungeon scenes and the dressmaker's dummy tied to the railings of an iron bedstead on the beach in *Glissements progressifs du plaisir*, the angel of death astride her motorcycle in *La Belle captive*.

Robbe-Grillet was a painter from a young age, so it is hardly surprising that colour and the visual should be among his major concerns, or that specific artists and paintings should have inspired many of the scenarios of his films. *L'Eden* contains allusions to Paul Klee who lived in Tunisia where the narrative is located, and also to Piet Mondrian and Marcel Duchamp.

Moreover, there are many direct references to specific paintings in *L'Eden*. The *Eden* café set is made up essentially of Mondrian paintings, and especially Marcel Duchamp's *Nude Descending a Staircase, No. 2*. The main character, the stranger is called Duchemin, itself a deformation of Duchamp. He himself is a painter. Again, Robbe-Grillet is happy to throw light on these choices:

> The reference to Duchamp comes from the fact that this painter, this creator, who is called Duchemin or Dutchman in the film, does paintings that, in fact, are not really paintings. They are scenes from life, compositions in which he mixes human figures, pieces of metal, doors, and similar items. Here then is an evident reference to techniques that exist in painting today, ever since Duchamp [...] Rather than being a direct reference to Duchamp's work, mine is a reference to Marcel Duchamp, the artist, and to his legacy of pop art, particularly to Rosenquist, Rauschenberg, and Jasper Johns. Dutchman/Duchemin, the character, is Duchamp, as I have said, and yet there is a very strong

reference to one Duchamp painting, his *Nude Descending a Staircase, No 2*, in which a nude character is at the same time on all of the steps at once. References to that painting occur in the film during a sequence where the spectator sees a whole series attributed to this Dutchman, such as women opening doors and going through doorways. There is an actual nude descending a staircase, and in the same reference, after the heroine finds the Dutchman in Tunisia, the viewer sees the works of the painter in question incorporated into the rest of the narrative. One might also recognize allusions to Duchamp's ready-made sculpture *The Large Glass* found in the Philadelphia Museum of Art. A remarkable work! It consists of a plate of glass and inside three things: *The Bride Stripped Bare by Her Bachelors, Even; Nine Malic Molds*; and *The Chocolate Grinder*. Such a reference can be addressed to a specialist and not at all to the larger film audience. I once wrote to a friend who is a specialist on Duchamp telling him that *Eden and After* was *my Large Glass*. (Fragola and Smith 1992: 62–3)

L'Eden is especially influenced by colour, a preoccupation which even extends to a certain discriminatory taste for some colours as opposed to others. He detested the colour green in Eastmancolor, one reason for his choice of location for *L'Eden*. He knew that on the island of Djerba at the time, only blue and white were allowed to be used for houses. In this, he was influenced by Paul Klee: 'It has to do with the relationship of Klee with Tunisia. He shared with Mondrian and me the fact that he did not like the color green, and Tunisia represented for me [...] a country without green' (ibid.: 62). 'The whole country' says Robbe-Grillet 'is blue and white. In the dry season, there is not a trace of green. This is something that really affected me from a sensual point of view' (quoted by Gardies 2005: 141).

In *La Belle captive*, he uses images from the paintings of Magritte and Manet to generate narrative. He had first used this title for a book containing reproductions of Magritte's paintings, including a number entitled *La Belle captive* (Fragola and Smith 1992: 16). Manet caused a scandal in his time with his painting *The Execution of Maximillian*, which we see several times in this film, and which shocked art critics of the period who found it cold and unfeeling. Robbe-Grillet explains the function of painting:

> more as a generator [...] than as an object of reflection [...] It is a legend that has been taken up by many writers, in particular by Goethe and Michelet. I have the impression that legends like this are important because they traverse our entire civilisation. In the film, the myth

of the young woman is shown in two aspects, one aspect being the captive, the girl who is simply the object of male desire. When the young man finds her, she has her hands chained behind her back, and he takes her to a room that resembles a cell. But in the room, she suddenly is no longer chained, and it is she who possesses the man.[2] (Ibid.: 103–4)

Shot/sequence

Robbe-Grillet's privileging of the visual and his fondness for the still tableau are also evident in his technical approach to filming. His approach to *L'Immortelle* was entirely different from the *Marienbad* concept and quite novel. Most strikingly, and perhaps in homage to the first silent films of Eisenstein, Robbe-Grillet decided on a bold and technically challenging departure from customary practice. Eisenstein had rejected the theory of montage as linking narrative sequences, basing his own approach instead on the succession of individual shots. Following Eisenstein, Robbe-Grillet thus attempts to privilege the image of the shot as the basic unit of film narrative. For Fragola and Smith, the spectator must therefore view each individual shot as if it were a painting, and spectator response should take place at a sensory and aesthetic rather than any rational level (ibid.: 6–7).[3]

This approach, however, caused problems during the shooting of *L'Immortelle* (1963) which was Robbe-Grillet's directorial debut, and he did not have the confidence to stand up to the crew who were unsympathetic to his technical innovations. Despite the growth at that time in France of an 'auteur' tradition, according to which the director was regarded as in sole charge of a film, Robbe-Grillet always felt that he was prevented by the technicians working with him from achieving all of his artistic aims.

A shot right at the beginning of the film illustrates this failure. The main character, a professor newly arrived in Istanbul and disoriented in these strange surroundings was to be shot in a darkened room whose windows looked out onto the Bosporus, gleaming brilliantly in the midday sun. Robbe-Grillet had intended that the only light in

2 Robbe-Grillet borrows the legend of 'The Bride of Corinth' in his third 'roman-esque', *Les derniers jours de Corinth*.

3 Taking the shot rather than the sequence as the basic unit of film determines his approach to both shooting and editing, as we shall see in Chapter 6.

the shot would come through the half-open slats of a blind at these windows. The actor was to stand at the window, facing outwards, his silhouette alone visible in the rays of light coming through the blind. Whereas Robbe-Grillet wanted no other light source in the room itself, since this would cast the actor's shadow onto the blind, the light-operator insisted that it was impossible to film the shot without internal lighting. The result was as Robbe-Grillet imagined it would be, and in his artistic terms, the shot is not a success (2005: 208–9). This perceived failure was a particular source of regret for him, since he had intended the shot to serve as the generating cell of the entire film. Robbe-Grillet himself provides a useful definition of this term, fundamental to an understanding of his cinema as a whole:

> When you abandon the entire notion of narration [...] then the question immediately arises as to the origin of the story. What is the place, the point, from which this story is produced? The question is an important one in many modern films that do not claim to be realistic. In *L'Immortelle*, in particular, the discourse originates from the character in the room who is thinking. The room must be dark, and the outside world should be very bright because what unfolds in his imagination lies beyond the confines of his room. (Fragola and Smith 1992: 29)

Another of Robbe-Grillet's attempts at technical innovation at the visual level met with the stubborn resistance of the continuity girl whose traditional notions were not shared by her director. Robbe-Grillet wanted to transgress a basic rule of cinematography, according to which a character moving in one shot should still be seen moving in the following shot: 'A un moment de mon script, l'acteur Jacques Doniol-Valcroze devait traverser toute la maison, et on le retrouvait brusquement assis à son bureau. Je voulais couper pendant qu'il montait l'escalier, un pied en l'air, et on devait le retrouver immobile'[4] (2005: 210). In the end, Robbe-Grillet achieved his aim of finding the actor sitting motionless immediately after the shot of him in motion by making adroit cuts in the editing process. The effect is somewhat disturbing and one that perfectly fits a narrative pervaded by a strong sense of strangeness. It is moreover an effect that was created

4 'At one point in my script, the actor Jacques Doniol-Valcroze was supposed to cross the entire house, and was suddenly to be found seated at his desk. I wanted to cut while he was climbing the stairs, one foot in the air, and have him found motionless.'

experimentally, as it were – a process increasingly typical of Robbe-Grillet's film-making method: 'Cette jeune femme à qui je n'arrivais pas à faire passer mes idées m'avait dit: «C'est exactement comme s'il y avait deux acteurs, comme si Doniol-Valcroze s'était dédoublé, et qu'on le voie en train de marcher vers lui-même, déjà assis.» J'ai trouvé cela formidable!'[5] (ibid.: 211).

Improvisation and the unexpected

Ultimately, Robbe-Grillet's approach to both the visual and, as we shall see, to the sound dimension of film is an essentially experimental one in the very real sense of this word, because he is constantly open to chance discoveries. He learned to improvise according to changing circumstances during the shooting of *L'Immortelle*. At the same time, he learned accordingly to prepare a script more flexibly and in far less detail, so as to facilitate such improvisations during the filming process. One of his favourite visual shots in the film arose precisely by pure chance. As the film was officially Turkish, and shot under the protection of the Turkish police, he was able to have streets and squares cleared for filming. For one particular scene, he had evacuated the square in front of the Fatih Camii mosque. A high tower had been constructed in order to position the camera for 'god shots'. Before the shooting could start, he was informed by the police that he must wait until a funeral procession had passed through the square. Since it was the funeral of a senior officer in the Turkish army, the police did not have the authority to stop the procession. As the procession began to cross the square, he nevertheless took the decision to shoot. The result was the shot of a sculptured wooden coffin, carried by six officers in full military uniform. In a film in which everything takes place in the hero's mind, the shot works well as a visual metaphor for his unspoken thoughts at that moment: the unknown woman he has met has disappeared and he is convinced that she must be dead. The absence of any sound in the shot helps to create the impression of a phantom coffin (ibid.: 212–13).

5 'This young woman whom I could not get to understand my ideas had said to me: "It's exactly as if there were two actors, as if Doniol-Valcroze had split in two and we saw see him walking towards another self that is already seated." I found that a wonderful idea!'

A similar opportunity arose during the shooting of *Un bruit qui rend fou* (1995). The film was shot on the Greek island of Hydra, which was full of cats. As one particular scene was being shot, a black cat appeared and started to follow one of the actors. The director decided to keep the shot because the cat added something special to the scene (ibid.: 212).

Such experiences of the unplanned event taught Robbe-Grillet that, unlike the novel, films go through not one but three creative stages: script-writing, shooting and editing, and that stages two and three are just as important artistically as stage one. Editing in particular which is a far less costly process than shooting he found to offer a quiet opportunity for contemplative creation. It is, above all, this continuous process of invention in cinema that distinguishes the third art from novel-writing, which is why Robbe-Grillet insisted that, unlike Eric Rohmer or François Truffaut, for example, he is not simply a novelist who makes films (ibid.: 213–14).

The audial

In spite of his initial resistance to the use of sound, Robbe-Grillet came to regard the soundtrack as a creative component of film, less a self-indulgence than a superdetermination: 'In a traditional film, the soundtrack is redundant, for it adds nothing to the meaning, nor does it even reinforce meaning; it is the same meaning. Whereas here, on the contrary, sound is itself a meaning, one related to the image, but that is never redundant' (Fragola and Smith 1992: 79). Sound in film is only noticed by viewers if it is directly linked to the image, whereas in his own cinema, there is a conscious intention to divorce the two in order to create an artistically motivated dissonance, a metaphor for the absence of meaning in an absurd world containing little coherence and few causal links (Robbe-Grillet 2005: 216–17).

However, he could not explore this concept properly until he came to direct *L'Immortelle*.[6] From *L'Immortelle* onwards until the 1980s film, *La Belle captive*, Robbe-Grillet was able to work with a more congenial sound engineer, Michel Fano, the brother of one of the former film's

6 The soundtrack he had planned for *Marienbad* was in fact modified by Resnais, who wanted to employ Delphine Seyrig's brother who was a musician: see Chapter 1.

producers, Jacques Fano. Michel Fano waited until after shooting to record sounds and noises that he felt he could use. At this early stage, the more experimental approach favoured by both sound-man and director was still rather tentative, and *L'Immortelle* does contain some conventional film music. The most interesting instances of this background music are probably the Turkish music and songs which are thematically related to the atmosphere and diegesis of the film.[7]

Three years later, the 1966 film, *Trans-Europ-Express* displays a particularly innovative use of sound as theme. In this first real exercise in game-playing, Jean, an author-filmmaker, boards the Trans-Europ-Express at the Gare du Nord in Paris en route for Antwerp with Marc, the film producer, and Lucette, Jean's assistant. They decide to make a film with the train as setting. The film is ostensibly, then, about its own making, but it is equally a parody of the stereotypes in thrillers published in popular magazines of the kind Jean buys at the station. Playing with themes of drug-smuggling, spying, prostitution and murder, the narrative mixes appearance and 'reality' in the style of such thrillers. At another level, it interrogates the very notion of authorship – Robbe-Grillet may well have had *Marienbad* in mind here – by having two of the film's characters, Jean-Louis Trintignant playing himself and Elias, a character imagined by him, 'assuming' responsibility for the narrative. William F. Van Wert comments:

> The 'plot' of the film is a pretext for Robbe-Grillet to expose the process of fiction, including the viewer in the decisions to remake a scene or to eliminate another scene [...] What is cast into doubt in the film is the 19th-century notion of the finished work of art from an omniscient author. That notion [...] is replaced by the notion of the 'game', in and for itself, with no significance outside the work of art. (Van Wert 1977: 28)

The film soundtrack is seen to have an essential role in the game, as we are cheekily confronted with an ironic *mise en abyme* of the role of sound in film. In the train compartment in which much of the action occurs, a tape recorder, operated by Robbe-Grillet, provides the sound, and is replayed from time to time to remind the trio what they have recorded. Through the window can be seen images of what is to be on screen. The compartment is therefore a 'cinematographic machine', a box in which the imaginary of the author can develop,

---

7 On the status and thematic role of Turkish music in the film, see Chapter 4.

and the film narrative alternates between an imagined film and what the imagination leads to, an abysmal echo of the dialogue between sound and vision (Castant 2005: 80–1). This self-referential structure draws attention to the purely artificial connection between the two media in film. Contradiction and self-referentiality can thus become in Robbe-Grillet's work the source of a creative soundtrack. Since, as a modern full-length film-maker, he is obliged to include sound, he turns this obligation into opportunity, and in fact, continues to privilege the visual by undermining conventional uses of the soundtrack. This leads to an extremely innovative use of sound as disjunctive from rather than complementary to film's visual imagery.

He had already recognised such possibilities when working on the *Marienbad* script, although they were not always realised by the director:

> I wanted Resnais to introduce these contradictions between sound and image [...] He did it timidly [...] I wanted the man's footsteps always to be on gravel, even when he was on carpeting, and the woman's footsteps always to be on carpeting, even when we saw her on gravel, which explains that in the park she twists her foot because the sound does not correspond to the image. Resnais said that the public would not understand. (Fragola and Smith 1992: 161)

Gilles Deleuze explains in detail the artistic intentions behind the soundtrack's contrapuntal role:

> In [*Marienbad*], and in all his work, Robbe-Grillet put into play a new asynchrony, where the talking and the visual were no longer held together, no longer corresponded, but belied and contradicted themselves, without it being possible to say that one rather than the other is 'right' [...] The visual and the talking may in each case take over the distinction between the real and the imaginary, sometimes one, sometimes the other, or the alternative of the true and the false; but a sequence of audio-visual images necessarily makes the distinct indiscernible, and the alternative undecidable [...][The voice-off] has lost the omnipotence which characterized it in the first stage of the talkie. It has ceased to see everything; it has become questionable, uncertain, ambiguous, as in Robbe-Grillet's *The Man Who Lies* [...] because it has broken from its moorings with the visual images which delegated to it the omnipotence which they lacked. The voice-off loses its omnipotence but by gaining autonomy. This is the transformation comprehensively analyzed by Michel Chion, and which led Bonitzer to propose the notion of 'voice-off-off'. (1989: 250)

As in *Trans-Europ-Express*, *L'Homme qui ment* (1968) unpicks the
nature and status of both dialogue and sound effects in establishing
meaning. The film opens with the noise of gunfire and shots of a
young man running through a forest, apparently pursued by Nazi
soldiers, but this pursuit is intercut with shots of a game of blind
man's buff, played by three beautiful women in a chateau. The man
appears to be hit by a bullet, then gets up and begins to narrate direct
to camera, identifying himself as Jean Robin or as Boris Varissa. Fano,
the sound recordist, was able to pick up interesting sounds which
had no connection with the shots being filmed, but his aim was to
organise these sounds into a kind of music. Thus, at the beginning of
the film, machine-gun shots are synchronised with shots of treetops,
producing a disturbing contrapuntal effect. Fano sees such effects in
geometrical terms:

> Il y a des sons horizontaux [...] des sons longs, tenus, un peu brouillés
> et, au contraire, des sons ponctuels comme les percussions et, entre
> les deux, un troisième genre, des sons que j'appelle itératifs, c'est-à-
> dire le picvert, la mitraillette. Cela fait trois types de sons très définies
> qui viennent jouer très précisément avec les structures verticales ou
> horizontales dans l'image.[8] (Gallet 1982: 37)

The shots are inspired by the storytelling of Boris, both improvising
and inventing how he came to meet Jean Robin. The rest of the film,
played out in the inn of the nearby town and the chateau itself, self-
consciously teases the spectator with contradictions and inconsis-
tencies that challenge Boris's account of a past friendship with Jean
Robin. Robbe-Grillet's project thus depends largely on dialogue as
well as sound effects:

> Robbe-Grillet notes that Boris Varissa is a mixture of the Don Juan
> myth and the various myths of the mad king and usurper king,
> especially that of Boris Goudonov [...] that Boris is someone who talks
> in order to construct his character, his past, his reality. He doesn't lie,
> he just talks, building his own credibility/reality with his words. There
> can be no truth or lie if there is no God, and Boris is someone who
> chooses to invent himself, to take the place of God. (Van Wert 1977: 31)

8 'There are horizontal sounds [...] long, sustained and somewhat confused
sounds, and on the other hand, isolated sounds like percussion, and in between
the two, a third category, sounds that I call iterative, like the woodpecker and
the machine-gun. That makes three well defined types of sound which can very
precisely accompany vertical or horizontal structures in the image.'

Voice thus participates fully in the narrative. But voice also operates as a destabilising element when finally everything is inverted. The image of Jean Robin replaces that of Boris on screen whereas it is filmed with the latter's voice. In *L'Homme qui ment*, speech is claimed to function as an act.[9] Robbe-Grillet himself explains:

> Je me rappelle que, à la sortie en salles de *L'Homme Qui Ment*, les critiques et le public ont dit que ce n'était pas un bon film, parce qu'ils n'arrivaient pas à savoir quand le personnage central mentait et quand il disait la vérité. Or, c'est la preuve même de l'incompréhension de base du public. Le film s'intitule *L'Homme Qui Ment*, mais en fin de compte il ne ment pas, il invente simplement à chaque instant sa propre existence par sa propre parole. Celle-ci est créatrice de sens, il peut dire une chose et son contraire ensuite, mais il faut le suivre dans ces méandres-là, comme s'il était une pure liberté existentielle, ne vivant autrement que par ce qu'il dit. C'est d'ailleurs pour cela que j'avais plus ou moins placé le récit sous le patronage de Don Juan que Kierkegaard a si longuement analysé: il est probablement le premier personnage de la littérature occidentale à avoir choisi sa propre parole comme vérité du monde, contre la parole de Dieu. C'est ce qu'on appelle un libertin.[10] (Robbe-Grillet 2005: 79)

L'Homme qui ment may therefore be said to express an existentialist view of identity as constantly recreating itself, and in this respect may have been influenced by the work of Sartre, as well as Kierkegaard and Heidegger (ibid.: 61–8). The philosophical underpinning of this technique is certainly interesting, but the overall effect of speech in this film is to destabilise the very construction of meaning in language

9 Deleuze makes this point on a number of occasions in his study of time in the cinema, referring to what he calls 'a to-and-fro between speech and image' (1989: 247, n. 46, 260 and 326, n. 46).

10 'I recall that, as they left the cinema after watching *The Man Who Lies*, critics and public said that it wasn't a good film because they couldn't work out when the main character was lying and when he was telling the truth. It is this very reaction that demonstrates the public's incomprehension. The film is entitled *The Man Who Lies*, but actually he does not lie, he simply invents his own existence at each moment through his own language. It is this that creates meaning. He can say one thing and then its opposite, but you have to follow him down those paths as if he were pure existential freedom, living only by what he says. Moreover, this is why I had in a way placed the narrative under Don Juan's patronage, a figure analysed in such detail by Kierkegaard. He is probably the first character in Western literature to have chosen his own language as truth of the world against the word of God. This is what we call a libertine.'

rather than to use language to create new meanings that are barely perceptible to the average audience.

In this film, sound also produces meaning indirectly, and therefore in more subtle ways. Michel Fano has explained how meaning may be constituted by a soundtrack:

> Une scène du début du film est tout à fait exemplaire à cet égard. Trintignant se tient avec les trois filles en haut d'un escalier, puis on a la scène au bord du puits où il raconte son histoire. Et juste avant qu'il tourne la tête (il y a souvent ce mouvement dans ce film), on entend déjà ce qu'on reconnaîtra par la suite comme le bruit de la chaîne du puits ou du seau qui heurte la margelle. Il y a, à mon sens, une sorte de télescopage du temps à cet endroit-là: on voit la servante avec les deux autres filles qui assistent à cet interrogatoire, on ne la voit pas partir et on la revoit après, en bas, dans le puits. Donc, j'ai voulu accentuer cet effet de sens par des sons du puits qu'on ne devrait entendre, en fait, qu'à la scène suivante. C'est un exemple parmi d'autres dans ce film de la polysémie qu'est *L'Homme qui Ment*.[11] ('Entretien avec Michel Fano', in Prédal (ed.) 2005: 88)

The sound of breaking glass is a repeated motif in *L'Homme qui ment*, *L'Eden* and *Glissements progressifs du plaisir* (1974), and there are frequently links in these films between sounds. At the end of *Glissements*, for example, successive sounds – organ, gunshots, bells, music, voices – mingle, transforming each other, and making up what Robbe-Grillet and Fano term the 'sensorial density' of the film.

Glissements repeats the motif of the broken glass which was already present in *Marienbad* and *L'Immortelle*. This motif works aesthetically at the level of both sight and sound. Lighting in all cases helps to produce a shimmering effect, as if reflecting the beauty of the woman with whom the motif is associated, while the equally pleasing sound

---

11 'A scene at the beginning of [*L'Homme qui ment*] is a good example: Trintignant is standing at the top of a staircase with three girls, then there is the scene at the edge of the well where he tells his story. And just before he turns his head (a frequent movement in the film), we hear the sound of the chain of the well or of the bucket knocking against the kerbstone. There is a sort of telescoping of time at that point: we see the serving-girl with the two others present at this cross-examination, we don't see her leave, and we see her again later down by the well. In this way, I wanted to draw attention to this meaningful effect by introducing sounds of the well which should not normally be heard until the following scene. It is one example among many in this film of the polysemy that is *L'Homme qui ment*.'

made by the glass breaking takes a variety of interesting forms in all three films, although many of these are practically imperceptible to the average spectator. For example, in *Glissements*, the heroine smashes a glass that resembles the holy grail, a vessel containing the sacred blood of Christ. This violent breakage is accompanied by a noise that was synthesised in the studio to produce a series of different notes, resembling the theme of the Grail in Wagner's *Parsifal* (Robbe-Grillet 2005: 219–21). However, these sounds are so delicate that few spectators have ever made the connection with Wagner's opera, and one is forced to wonder whether an artistic effect that does not communicate itself to its audience is little more than authorial narcissism.

Similarly, during another scene in this film in which the female lawyer is questioning her young female client, increasingly loud noises are heard coming through the barred windows of her cell, such that at times their conversation becomes almost inaudible. While these external sounds, unlike those of the previous example, are certainly in evidence, their origins never could be unless this were expressly revealed, for they are the sounds of the guillotine being constructed in a prison yard which Claude Lelouche had recorded for one of his films. As her lawyer warns her of the seriousness of a murder charge, the heroine replies with childlike innocence: 'Je peux dire n'importe quoi, de toute façon on ne guillotine pas les petites filles.'[12] In this case, then, there is a direct link between the dialogue and these sound effects, but again, since the audience could never be aware of it, its artistic status is questionable. Robbe-Grillet himself takes this hidden effect even further by adding a whistling sound, which he imagines to be made by one of the workmen building the guillotine. This man appears to whistle the beginning of Wagner's *Tristan and Isolde*, the song of the boatman taking Isolde back to King Marc. This whistling sound is noticeable, and some may recognise its origins in Wagner, yet since it manifestly appears to have no connection with the scene in which it is found, spectators have thought it to be external to the film itself, and in one case, retailed by Robbe-Grillet, a sound made by the projectionist! (ibid.: 220–1).

Robbe-Grillet and Fano are probably most successful in their use of barely perceptible sounds to evoke a subtle eroticism, the play between the hidden and the visible, between absence and presence

---

12 'I can say whatever I like anyway because they don't guillotine young girls.'

being both the origin and the essence of eroticism in a Freudian perspective.[13]

In *Trans-Europ-Express*, for example, when he has killed Eva, Elias is heading towards the Eve cabaret when he hears footsteps in the street which symbolically suggest a sexual scenario. Footsteps also function erotically in other films: the sound of a woman's footsteps on a spiral staircase in *L'Homme qui ment*, and the sound of high heels in *La Belle captive*. Other suggestive sounds like whispering, or deep breathing, or the touch of cloth when, in *L'Homme qui ment*, young women play blind man's buff, or the light tread of a woman in this film can have similar effects, provided that they are pointed to the audience by a visual or a dialogic cue, for example: 'Vous avez entendu ce bruit?' says Boris in *L'Homme qui ment*. 'Le bruit d'une nonne qui court dans la forêt.'[14]

Music

Music in some cases structures the film in which it is found, functioning as a thematic generator, for instance in *Le Jeu avec le feu* (1975), in which *The Flying Dutchman* provides the essential scaffolding. More often, though, the music that Robbe-Grillet favours is itself as cacophonous as his sound effects, and as with sound, it frequently has an effect that is contrapuntal to the meaning apparently associated with the visual imagery. In *L'Eden*, this relationship between music and image is made transparent: students improvise a music with cups, trays and teapots. Music develops here from the combination of sounds thus produced, but there is frequently a discontinuity between sound and image. In *Glissements*, for example, shots of Alice in a trio of musicians seem quite unrelated to the rest of the film. Alexandre Castant argues that these images suspend the

13 See Sigmund Freud's theory of the 'Fort! Da!' game (1984 [1920]). Freud's notion of 'Fort! Da!' has its origins in his analysis of a game played by his grandchild with a cotton bobbin, and which he interprets as a symbolic enactment of the mother's presence and absence. The repetition of the 'Gone! Here!' gesture would in this interpretation be motivated by an unconscious need to master the mother's absence and thus to come to terms with it. See also Roland Barthes's notion of textual striptease as a play between the visible and the hidden (1973: 19).

14 'Did you hear that noise? [...] The noise of a nun running through the forest.'

narrative, isolating the soundtrack in the flow of narration (2005: 79). Such effects can be puzzling, but puzzlement is no doubt what Robbe-Grillet intended, impeding the reception of a comprehensible linear narrative.

Robbe-Grillet's use of *La Traviata* in *Trans-Europ-Express* is possibly the best example in his films of an attack on the conventional use of music as the servant of film continuity (ibid.: 79–80). When he came to work on this film, Fano took the technique of contrapuntal sound much further than before. The soundtrack includes snatches of Verdi's opera, yet so subtly done as to be practically imperceptible. Michel Fano talks about 'musical collages' in the film, and Robbe-Grillet explains the use of Verdi instead of Wagner in terms of the ease of using snatches of the music (Gallet 1982: 22–3). At times, fairly long sections of music are recognisable, but at other times, there is just a series of chords, or even a single one. The inclusion of this music was purely ludic, a joke for the cognoscenti. Robbe-Grillet explains: 'La Traviata [...] is the story of a woman of a good family who becomes a whore, who has gone off course or off the right track. Then there are all those railroad tracks [*voies* in French], and the story itself which leaves the right track for a perverse one' (Fragola and Smith 1992: 39).

Another extremely subtle form of *musique concrète* accompanies at times the Verdi music in this film. For example, Robbe-Grillet recalls that in the train, there is a moment when symphonic variations on the noise of the air conditioning can be heard, but even he admits that they are audible only by those with very acute hearing:

> si, après l'avoir enregistré avec soin, on travaille ce souffle sur une machine électronique, on peut très bien en faire sortir sinon des notes, du moins des bruits complexes [...] Ces variations symphoniques sur le bruit de l'air conditionné, je les ai entendues une seule fois, au studio d'enregistrement, mais jamais en salle. Ce sont des choses trop fines.[15] (2005: 216–17)

In *Trans-Europ-Express*, as elsewhere, then, the use of Verdi is partly a humorous one, aimed at parodying the link between incidental music and visuals, and Verdi works well from this point of view because his music does not seem designed to produce its intended

---

15 'if, having carefully recorded everything, you work on this breath of music on an electronic machine, you can easily create, if not notes, at least complex sounds [...] I heard these symphonic variations on the air conditioning just once in the recording studio, but never in the cinema. These sounds are too subtle.'

effects. In Verdi, a tense, dramatic scene is often accompanied by upbeat music. In this way, too, Robbe-Grillet attacks the stereotypes of musical accompaniment in film (Gallet 1982: 23).

Many such effects are achieved in the editing room. Robbe-Grillet explains how music is often used in a trial-and-error fashion during the editing process:

> When I use recorded music as massively as *La Traviata* in *Trans-Europ-Express* or a Schubert quartet in *La Belle Captive*, I have at the beginning an idea that it will work out. But when the scenes are acted out, there is no music [...] it is during the editing that we try to see if it might work. (Fragola and Smith 1992: 110)

This approach sometimes produced unexpected results. For example, he wanted to use Schubert's 14th quartet, *Death and the Maiden* for *La Belle captive* because of the title, but when he tried it out during editing, it did not work. His wife, Catherine suggested he try the 15th quartet which worked very well (ibid.).

In the case of Verdi's *La Traviata* in *Trans-Europ-Express*, Robbe-Grillet also cut the music into fragments in the editing room to suit the visuals: 'we used chords, just chords or a series of chords, which were then cut on the sound tape and were later synchronized with the image. It is great fun to adapt music to the image and then to rectify the music as a function of the image, which cannot, after all, be cut at random' (ibid.: 40).

Musical sounds, then, are often used for artistic effect in these films in quite unconventional ways, but in *L'Eden* it is the very structures of music that are harnessed to determine the film's sequentiality. *L'Eden* was the first of Robbe-Grillet's films where most of the script was not written in advance. All the actors knew was that they were going to spend a month in Czechoslovakia and a month on Djerba. It was shot according to a grid whose cells are formed by the intersection of twelve themes and ten narrative series, much akin to the structures of Arnold Schoenberg's atonal music. Robbe-Grillet provides the clearest explanation of this approach:

> The point was to produce narrative by using a system of relationships between scenes that seemed the most opposed to the notion of narrative. The narrative relationship between scenes is normally one of causality; that is, the scenes are related to each other in a chain of cause and effect. In *Eden*, on the other hand, the scenes succeed each other in the order of seriality; that is, the elements of the scenes were

grouped according to series – roughly in the sense that Schoenberg used in twelve-tone music. I chose twelve recognizable themes: the theme of poison, the theme of fire, etc. Just as Schoenberg would use twelve chromatic tones in a series and then use the same twelve tones in a different order in subsequent series, I planned to use the twelve themes in a series and then the same twelve themes in a newly ordered series and so on. When tones are grouped together, no meaning is produced, but when the theme 'to drink' is juxtaposed to the theme 'poison', it produces 'drink poison'. The combination thus produces the theme of 'death'. I wrote only the first series. All the other series were produced by the work itself and the adventure of the shooting [...] Along with the credits of the film for *Eden*, there is what might be called a thematic set of credits. One hears a voice that presents the themes of the film accompanied by images. Thus the credits are both imagistic and vocal. In particular, there is a presentation of the twelve themes that organize the film. (Ibid.: 55–7)

However, these twelve themes are not perceivable in the finished work, and even Robbe-Grillet himself cannot identify them: 'The serial system was a generating system, and then it disappeared exactly as a scaffolding would when building a cathedral' (ibid.: 57). One is bound to wonder, therefore, whether this imperceptible structure can be regarded as little more than another authorial joke.[16]

Apart from such artistic innovations, it also amuses Robbe-Grillet to go against the grain in other respects, and again to allow chance to determine the result. He speaks of the use of *La Traviata* in *Trans-Europ-Express*:

Verdi had just fallen into the public domain so we had the right to use his music but not the mechanical reproductions of his music. So I used a Russian recording. They do not worry about authors' rights since they, at least at that time, had not signed the international copyright convention. They publish my books without sending me royalties because they have not signed the convention, so I took great pleasure in using a Soviet recording. Moreover, I find it amusing that she is singing in Russian. (Ibid.: 39)

16 In *Le Jeu avec le feu*, Robbe-Grillet used three sound stereotypes in similar fashion: a German military march, a Brazilian samba and a fragment from Verdi's *Il Trovatore*. These three musical elements formed the basis of the whole structure of the film (Gallet 1982: 23). Again, it seems unlikely that spectators would be aware of this structure. The musical structure of *L'Eden et après* is discussed in more detail in Chapter 3.

Some concluding remarks

Robbe-Grillet's use of sound and musical effects is, unsurprisingly then, of a piece with his identity as a modern artist – there are similarities here with the American artist, Rauschenberg – for whom improvisation, spontaneity and the random selection of disparate objects and sounds creates new meanings. As we have seen, these aspects of his filmic work are not merely peripheral adjuncts to a core narrative, but an indispensible part of the creative act. Whether or not they are appreciated by the audience will depend to a large extent on the erudition and perceptiveness of the individual spectator, and it seems unlikely that most would identify the origins of the sound effects employed. Use of music will no doubt be more successful, although there are notable exceptions. In the end, the visual and audial scaffolding of the films is probably best experienced on a sensorial rather than an intellectual level. This is, after all, the level at which all art, whether modern or traditional, aims to achieve its most enduring impact.

References

Artaud, Antonin (1964), *Le Théâtre et son double*, coll. Idées, 114, Paris, Éditions Gallimard.

Barthes, Roland (1973), *Le Plaisir du texte*, Paris, Éditions du Seuil.

Castant, Alexandre (2005), 'Récit, figuration, imaginaire: La part du son chez Alain Robbe-Grillet', in Prédal, *Robbe-Grillet Cinéaste*, 79–85.

Deleuze, Gilles (1989), *Cinema 2: The Time Image*, London, Athlone Press.

Fano, Michel (2005), 'Entretien avec Michel Fano' ('Interview with Michel Fano') (2005), in Prédal, *Robbe-Grillet Cinéaste*, 87–90.

Fragola, Anthony N. and Smith, Roch C. (1992), *The Erotic Dream Machine: Interviews with Alain Robbe-Grillet on His Films*, Carbondale and Edwardsville, Southern Illinois University Press.

Freud, Sigmund (1984 [1920]), *Beyond the Pleasure Principle*, Harmondsworth, Penguin, Pelican Freud Library, vol. 11.

Gallet, Pascal-Emmanuelle (ed.) (1982), *Alain Robbe-Grillet: Œuvres Cinématographiques*, Édition vidéographique critique, Paris, Ministère des relations extérieures, Cellule d'animation culturelle.

Gardies, André (2005), 'Le travail du double', in Prédal, *Robbe-Grillet Cinéaste*, 105–43.

Prédal, René (2005), *Robbe-Grillet Cinéaste*, Études publiées sous la direction de René Prédal, Caen, Presses universitaires de Caen.

Robbe-Grillet (1963), 'Temps et description dans le récit d'aujourd'hui', in *Pour un nouveau roman*, Paris, Éditions de Minuit, 123–34.

Robbe-Grillet, Alain (2005), *Préface à une vie d'écrivain*, Paris, France Culture, Éditions du Seuil.

Van Wert, William F. (1977), *The Film Career of Alain Robbe-Grillet*, London, George Prior Publishers.

1 *L'Eden et après* (1971)

2 *La Belle captive* (1983)

3 *La Belle captive* (1983)

4 *Glissements progressifs du plaisir* (1974)

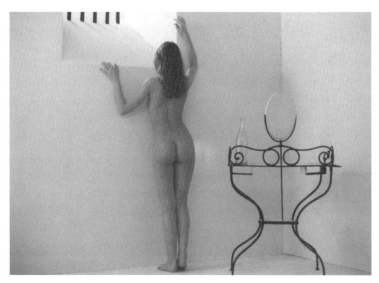

5 *Glissements progressifs du plaisir* (1974)

6 Alain Robbe-Grillet with Marie-France Pisier during the shooting of *Trans-Europ-Express* (1966)

7 Alain Robbe-Grillet with Jean-Louis Trintignant during the shooting of *Le Jeu avec le feu* (1974)

8 Alain Robbe-Grillet directing Gabrielle Lazure and Daniel Mesguich in *La Belle captive* (1983)

9 *L'Année dernière à Marienbad* (1961)

10 *L'Eden et après*
(1971)

11 Still from *Le Jeu avec le feu* (1975), with Philippe Noiret, representing a young woman in her bath reflected in a mirror

12 *L'Homme qui ment* (1968)

13 *Le Jeu avec le feu* (1975)

14 *Le Jeu avec le feu* (1975)

15 *L'Immortelle* (1963)

16 *L'Immortelle* (1963)

17 *L'Immortelle* (1963)

18 *L'Immortelle* (1963)

19 Alain Robbe-Grillet with Dimitri de Clercq during the shooting of *Un bruit qui rend fou* (1995), on the island of Hydra, 1994

20 *L'Immortelle* (1963)

3

Playtime: *L'Homme qui ment, L'Eden et après, N. a pris les dés, Le Jeu avec le feu, Un bruit qui rend fou*

Intertextuality as play

The repetition from film to film, and indeed between films and novels, of dominant themes and favoured locations in Robbe-Grillet's work taken as a whole creates an intertextual network within this author's corpus: doubling, borrowings from the film noir, circularity of structure, and particular sexual themes and motifs all form a body of cinematic work that justifies the label of auteur in the strict sense of this word. Ben Stoltzfus notes:

> reflection from one book or film to another. A brief allusion, (outside the work in which the object or motif first appears), to the voyeur's bicycle, the white Buick, doors, metal beds, prison cells, string, dismembered dolls, and the like become a 'mise en abyme' for [the original work]. Familiar names such as Boris, Franck, Franz, Marchat, Laura, Jacqueline recur with the frequency of mirrors, windows, pictures, stones and arabesques. Situations depicting or describing rape, blood, fire and aggression, like miniature mirrors in the paintings of Van Eyck, Memling and Metzys, reflect one work into another, creating a network of interrelated images linking the different parts with the body fiction. (1985: 100)

Indeed, there is a self-conscious playfulness in the ways in which Robbe-Grillet's novels and films return obsessively to the same themes and motifs. For example, he tells us that at the beginning of *N. a pris les dés* there is the seagull from *Le Voyeur* making figures of eight in the sky (Fragola and Smith 1992: 66). The brothel in *Un bruit qui rend fou* is called 'La Villa Bleue' ('The Blue Villa'), the same name as that of the brothel in the 1965 novel, *La Maison de rendez-vous*.

This intertextuality is not merely a characteristic but a theme, informing many important aspects of the filmic œuvre, and forming part of a ludic tendency shared by other exponents of the new novel (most notably, Robert Pinget and Raymond Queneau). Robbe-Grillet is conscious of this wider tendency among other authors of his generation, and in a sense pays homage to it in his own work. The ludicity of Robbe-Grillet's work does not stop, however, at the narcissistic self-mirroring of a personal or interpersonal intertextuality, but extends to the experimental use of game structures within the filmic work, and to their employment outside it as an approach to the making of the films themselves. The structures that Robbe-Grillet draws from expressionistic and pop art and from contemporary music, some examples of which were discussed in the previous chapter, may also be considered as expressions of a playful approach to art.

Theories of play

These ludic tendencies are in harmony, Robbe-Grillet argues, with theories of modern art in general which:

> accepts the idea of playing with the work [...] this playfulness is part of the creative process, and it is also part of the contact with the public. The work of art invites the audience to play with the film and beyond that, to play with their own lives. The situation is similar to the one announced by Hegel as being the end of history, the moment he calls 'the Sunday of life', where the free man begins to play with the world. (Fragola and Smith 1992: 58)

Critics have long since recognised the ludic nature of Robbe-Grillet's work, and linked it to this theoretical background. For Ira Kuhn (1976: 194), the notion of art as quest has always involved an element of playfulness, while for Bruce Morrissette, 'the proliferation of game structures [...] identifies him as a notable example of *artifex ludens* [...] It is even possible to reduce the numerous game structures to a few basic models, such as the circular or winding path of individual *cases* or rectangles (like those found on board games played with dice and pawns), the maze or labyrinth' (1966: 157–8).[1] Morrissette tells us that:

> Puzzles, mathematical games, riddles, paradoxes, topological curiosities (like the Möbius strip), optical illusions (like the pinhole fly image

1 We note that one of Robbe-Grillet's novels has the title, *Dans le labyrinthe* (1959).

in *Dans le labyrinthe*), and all such pararational phenomena have fasci-
nated Robbe-Grillet since childhood [...] His first project for a novel
[...] was to have its plot organized according to the hermetic series of
108 scales on drawings made by medieval alchemists of the legendary
snake Ouroboros. (Ibid.: 158)

Games as thematic content: spectator as player or detective

This playful tendency is particularly noticeable in *L'Homme qui ment*
with regard to the complete absence of any sure footing for the
spectator who cannot ever be certain that a given character is telling
the truth or lying. Deleuze's concept of the 'incompossible' discussed
in Chapter 1 abolishes the traditional distinction between true and
false, and is best illustrated in this film. Deleuze's analysis is worth
quoting in full:

> From the novel to the cinema, Robbe-Grillet's work testifies to the
> power of the false as principle of production of images [...] The images
> must be produced in such a way that the past is not necessarily true,
> or that the impossible comes from the possible. When Robbe-Grillet
> appeals to the detail which falsifies in the image (for instance, *The Man
> Who Lies* should not have the same suit and tie several years later), we
> see that the power of the false is also the most general principle that
> determines all the relationships in the direct time-image. In one world,
> two characters know each other, in another world they don't know each
> other, in another one the first knows the second, in another, finally, the
> second knows the first. Or two characters betray each other, only the
> first betrays the second, neither betrays, the first and second are the
> same person who betrays himself under two different names: contrary
> to what Leibnitz believed, all these worlds belong to the same universe
> and constitute modifications of the same story. Narration is no longer a
> truthful narration which is linked to real (sensory-motor) descriptions.
> Description becomes its own object and narration becomes temporal
> *and* falsifying at exactly the same time [...] All this could be summed up
> by saying that the forger becomes *the* character of the cinema: not the
> criminal, the cowboy, the psycho-social man, the historical hero, the
> holder of power, etc., as in the action-image, but the forger pure and
> simple, to the detriment of all action [...] he now assumes an unlimited
> figure which permeates the whole film. He is simultaneously the man
> of pure descriptions and the maker of the crystal-image, the indiscern-
> ibility of the real and the imaginary; he passes into the crystal, and

makes the direct time-image visible; he provokes undecidable alternatives and inexplicable differences between the true and the false, and
thereby imposes a power of the false as adequate to time, in contrast
to any form of the true which would control time. *The Man Who Lies*
is one of Robbe-Grillet's finest films: this is not a localized liar, but an
unlocalizable and chronic forger in paradoxical spaces. (1989: 131–2)

There is clearly a significant element of play in this scenario, which
repeats Robbe-Grillet's conception of the characters in *Marienbad*
inhabiting separate worlds that nevertheless belong to the same
universe. At the same time, of course, such a conception is in harmony
with the theories of quantum mechanics according to which we may
live in a 'multiverse' in which different universes offering different
experiences may coexist without contradiction.

In some of the films, characters themselves play games which may
be seen as mirroring the greater narrative. In *Marienbad*, for example,
play 'duplicates, at the level of the characters and within the fictional
field, the general pattern of the novel or film [...] All the games of
the film, including that of the shooting gallery, reinforce the themes
of contest, domination, imposition of one's will upon another, even
violence, that form the basis of the main action of *Marienbad*' (Morrissette 1966: 157–63).

Thus the Nim game is a *mise en abyme* of the central situation of
the narrative: 'The antagonists X and M confront each other in two
ways: in the struggle of passion to possess A, and in the duel of the
mind to win at Nim [...] M always wins, but he "can lose", as he says,
and in the end he does. Is it deliberately?' (ibid.: 163). Played between
X and M, it is a game which can be won and lost at the same time,
rather like the relationship between X and A which has no obviously
desirable outcome for either character.

L'Homme qui ment: games and the erotic

Childhood play and sexual discovery have clear links, in many
respects. For Melanie Klein (1949), play is a tool for ego integration
and the resolution of phantasies. Play, as the intermediate space
between fantasy and external reality, can be a means of resolving the
gap between the two and negotiating an intermediate space between
an unconscious and an external reality.

D. Winnicott also emphasises the importance of play in child development. The 'good enough' mother, according to Winnicott (1971), must make the child realise that reality is outside its ubiquitous grasp. In order to achieve this, the child must establish a relationship with a 'transitional object' that will inhabit this intermediate space between the unconscious and external reality, such as a toy or mannerism. As a space carved out between fantasy and the real, and as a fulcrum between an apparent external reality and the internal reality of the character (and the spectator), Robbe-Grillet's cinematic world is not dissimilar to Winnicott's 'transitional medium' as a means of achieving ego integration.

Thus, the game of blind man's buff, for example, at the beginning of *L'Homme qui ment*, allows the exploration of bodies under the guise of childhood play, but such games, it is implied, are never entirely innocent as the opening of this film intercuts scenes of young women in a chateau playing this game with shots of a man fleeing from armed soldiers in the forest. Both activities are versions of 'hide and seek', and the game played for fun inside by the women is clearly intended ironically to mirror the 'life and death' struggle of the men outside. The manner in which the women's game is played is highly eroticised, as the players touch each other sensually, their silence and the exchange of meaningful looks pregnant with an absent meaning. Later, when the man arrives at the chateau, the sudden presence of the masculine in an otherwise exclusively female environment, associated as it is with the more dangerous scenario in the forest, announces a narrative in which gender and the relations between the masculine and the feminine may be important themes. Having played versions of this game in their own childhood, the majority of spectators are no doubt able to identify with the memories this scene evokes, memories of the exploration of the other's body and the innocent sexuality to which it responds.

Similarly, the game structure of *Trans-Europ-Express*, according to which the narrative progresses in a series of starts, stops, retreats and new starts, may be said to reproduce the thrills and disappointments of childhood play in a manner that is humorous and artistically interesting. Robbe-Grillet has described this structure as that of the 'jeu de l'oie' or 'goose game'.[2] There are also faint echoes of

---

2 The 'royal goose game', a near British equivalent, was played in the eighteenth and nineteenth centuries. The modern children's board game, 'Snakes and Ladders', may be derived from these earlier games.

the therapeutic effects of such game structures which mirror the vicissitudes of life. A writer-director, played by the author himself is seated in a railway carriage with his continuity girl, played by his wife, Catherine, a sound-man and other technicians, 'imagining' a scenario that would suit a train journey. He first comes up with the stereotyped events of spy films, but quickly replaces these with more subtle storylines. Improvisation, then, not only informs the way the film is made, but is ironically reflected and commented on at every step of the process itself. Robbe-Grillet describes his role in the film as that of a 'contemporary archetype', a 'creator coming to grips with his creation as it takes shape' (quoted by Gardies 2005: 137). The game itself, its movements forwards, then back again, then forwards, and the running commentary upon it, thus tend to overshadow the fiction the game is designed to generate, and *Trans-Europ-Express* becomes in large part a self-conscious exercise in form.

L'Eden et après

L'Eden et après (1971) is possibly the most experimental of Robbe-Grillet's films, its narrative generated, as we shall see, in a random manner. This was, of all Robbe-Grillet's films, the one most open to 'invention'. Such a degree of improvisation makes this film, above all, an exercise in play: 'Not only was [*L'Eden*] not written in advance, of all of my films, it is the one that was the least written. Improvised is not a word I like to use, as you know, so let us say it was created collectively' (Fragola and Smith 1992: 58).

University students meet after class in a café called The Eden. This café is full of mirrors which appear to create illusion and deception, and is the stage upon which the students play games of violence, eroticism and death. The students come across as bored middle-class youth, inventing dangerous games to amuse themselves. One evening, a stranger, Duchemin/Dutchman arrives and becomes involved in their games, but things appear to take a sinister turn. He is significantly older than they are, but has a seductive appeal. He begins to tell them tales of Africa, and of its shimmering, dreamlike landscape. The most sensitive among them, Violette, agrees to meet him and other students at night. She is subsequently seen running through a deserted factory. The impression is that she has been set a task, and must achieve some sort of objective. She is hindered in this quest by whispers, cries and a series of disturbing encounters with her friends from the café. Eventually, she comes across the stranger at the appointed place, but he is dead. The young woman panics and looks in vain for her friends. When they all eventually reach the canal, the man has vanished. All Violette has is a postcard from Djerba, found on the man's corpse, bearing a laconic text which seems to contain an invitation to a secret rendezvous in Djerba, where she meets all her friends from the café and the Dutchman or his double, who here works as a sculptor of *tableaux vivants*, mingling the bodies of women and random, everyday objects. New trials await Violette in his house, on the sands, in the water, in fire, trials which Robbe-Grillet compares to those that confront Sade's Justine or the knights of the holy grail, including abduction and torture. One after another, these friends meet their end as a result of rivalry and revenge, including Dutchman himself who dies at a place that mirrors the canal of the first part of the narrative.

This film, which is possibly Robbe-Grillet's most referential in terms of a historical and social reality, to some extent reflects a contemporary drug culture. The 'powder of fear' which Violette is forced to take by Duchemin has effects similar to those of hallucinatory drugs such as LSD which generate an 'alternative' reality. It is, after all, taken in a 1970s student milieu, in which drug-taking was regarded as both a form of play and a means of stimulating creativity. Above all, however, the plot of *L'Eden* probably strikes the contemporary viewer as remarkably similar to the many interactive computer games, such as 'World of Warcraft' or 'Final Fantasy', currently played online, and in which the player must defeat a number of opponents in order to achieve an objective. Robbe-Grillet explains:

> A young woman goes through a series of ordeals. These ordeals resemble the ones found in novels of chivalry – cruel dangers must be overcome by the young knight. He triumphs little by little over these ordeals until the moment when an enemy steals from him the portion of his clothing or of his armor that protects him from evil. Lost in the forest without this essential article that protects him, he is effectively destined to die until the moment when he meets his double who returns the missing article. In this film, the young knight is a young woman, and the ordeals have, as they always have in this kind of narrative, a violent and sexual character. The protective object – I intended it to be humorous – is a miniskirt of the 1970s. Having lost

this dress – which was, in essence, her armor – she is on the point of perishing until the moment when, in the forest, which has now become the desert, she encounters her double who returns the dress. (Fragola and Smith 1992: 60–1)

The catalyst for the film narrative is a stolen painting which has to be retrieved, but as William F. Van Wert observes:

Behind the pretext is a questioning of the film's way of telling a story, especially in the discontinuous opening credits and titles, which present an 'inventory' of all the themes which come into play in this film-game. The characters play games in the film, but the spectator never learns the rules. Robbe-Grillet juggles appearances, surfaces, false doubles. He plays with time and space, with reality and the imaginary, with eroticism and allusions to art, with colors (the blue and white of the painting and of the Tunisian landscape, the red of blood and of the Café Eden). Robbe-Grillet is quoted as saying that he would like to replace the notions of 'profundity' and 'depth' in the work of art with the notion of the game. (1977: 165)

So, the film is not about the quest for a lost painting, nor the identity of a stranger, both of which are just pretexts for a sophisticated game taking place in two continents – if, indeed, the events that make up the game take place at all outside the young woman's imagination. Here, ludic structure is dominant over content more than in any of Robbe-Grillet's other cinematic works.

Game structure of *L'Eden et après*

In *L'Eden*, the causal chain of the traditional narrative is replaced by a series devoid of logical or chronological links. The film groups ten series: the credits, which list the themes of the narrative, the Eden café before the stranger's arrival, the hallucinations of the power of fear, Eden after the stranger's arrival, the factory, the film on Tunisia, the Tunisian village, the Dutchman's house, the prison, the mirages in the desert.

These ten series employ twelve themes: the painting, blood, the double, dancing, light, the labyrinth, the prison, viscous matter, eroticism in art, death, water, the doors. These themes produce stories to the extent that they are repeated several times in different contexts. The film is therefore the creation of a story which does not exist at the outset but which takes shape as a result of the organisation of the series. For instance, the little picture of a Tunisian house in blue and white becomes the catalyst for a whole series of adventures. In each of the series, the characters of the Eden Café (Frantz the waiter, the students, the stranger) reappear in different guises, but retain the main characteristics of their personality. Indeed, the concept of the double undermines any realist effect: the double poisoning of Boris, the double drowning of the stranger, the double dance of Violette and her encounter with her own double on the beach.[3]

The system of the series is itself undermined by two further incompatible systems: the trio of locations (Eden Café, factory, Tunisia), and the perception–fantasy duality based on two essential articulations: Violette's appearance in the film on Tunisia and the absorption of the Tunisian sky by the blue of the wall of the bedroom in the final sequence. These two visual images link reality and the imaginary, reinforced by a number of pictorial references: abstract paintings by the Dutch artist, Piet Mondrian, the *Nude Descending Staircase* of Marcel Duchamp, and other images by the Belgian surrealist, Paul Delvaux and the American pop artist, James Rosenquist.

As the film opens, students are playing strange erotic games, which might be described as psychodrama – scenes that were certainly sketched out beforehand but which Robbe-Grillet claims were also open to improvisation. These games, seven in total, constitute the first series. Only the first series was written in advance (Gallet 1982: 38). In the end, there were ten series rather than five, and twelve themes not seven – mirroring the twelve notes of Bach's scale which Schoenberg had exploited. These changes were obviously made during shooting, and so may well have been the result of some improvisation. However, the preciseness of such a structure cannot have been solely the product of random experimentation. Robbe-Grillet has claimed that he was not aware of the series (ibid.: 39) – he compares this structure to scaffolding like that used to build a medieval cathedral – but it is hard to believe that structures of such complexity could be unconsciously manipulated.

---

3 The theme of the double is a dominant one throughout Robbe-Grillet's corpus, and derives from literature and especially music, in which themes and motifs are often repeated with slight variations. The motif of the double, which has dream and fantasy connections, appeals to him in large part because it undermines Balzacian realism: see Robbe-Grillet 2005, ch. 10, 'Le goût du double', 87–95.

N. a pris les dés

This made-for-television film, a self-conscious pastiche of *L'Eden et après*, was shown one evening in 1975 on the French TV channel, FR3. The very making of this film is a piece of game-playing in itself. Made in 1971, the same year as *L'Eden*, the film features the same actors, and the script has a close relationship with the cinema film. The author explains:

> The title in French [...] is an anagram of *L'Eden et après*. I use considerable material from *Eden* in this film, but the beginning in particular differs from *Eden and After*. The second half of the film uses scenes from *Eden* because the producer did not want to underwrite further work. Yet the first part shows what the film might have been. It was an interesting experiment [...] While I made use of some of the same images as in *Eden*, I combined them differently and gave them a new sound. I also used the second takes – which are different and are always variants for me – plus the unused heads and tails of the *Eden* shots. The idea was to tell a completely different story, since the first one in *Eden* is serial and the second is aleatory. Serial and aleatory musical structures were in fashion in that period – the 1960s and 1970s [...] at the time there were fairly surprising experiments with aleatory music. Musicians on stage would throw dice in order to pick the score they would play [...] In *N Took the Dice*, Richard Leduc, who played Marc-Antoine in *Eden*, is now called N (as in narrator). He addresses the audience directly in a conventional fixed shot used for television commentators and throws the dice to find the next sequence of the film [...] Of course, nothing proves that I respected the game [...] Obviously, all it takes is to make a cut between the moment he throws the dice and the moment one sees the outcome in a close-up of the dice on the table to change that outcome. (Fragola and Smith 1992: 63–4)

N. a pris les dés is a clear intertextual echo of Stéphane Mallarmé's 1897 poem, 'Un coup de dés n'abolira jamais le hasard' ('One throw of the dice will never abolish chance'), and like Mallarmé's, a poetic exercise in the role played in art by randomness and multiple alternatives.[4] The title of this TV film thus immediately draws attention to play as a source of creativity. Whether or not Robbe-Grillet's film is championing the role of chance in creative activity, however, is left

---

4 Mallarmé's poem is on one level an exploration of how the disposition of words and spaces on the page impacts on the meanings of the work, and so like Robbe-Grillet's film, is essentially an exercise in form.

ambiguous. Indeed, the film appears to offer its audience different, even contradictory ideas. Towards the end of the film, N, the dice-thrower and source of an apparently random narration, declares: 'Mais le hasard a ses lois lui aussi, dit-on.'[5] The film then cuts to a mathematics class at the university, where a formula on the board which implies a random series instantly seems to undermine N.'s statement. Robbe-Grillet has maintained that he is here alluding to the theory of chance in mathematical statistics (Fragola and Smith 1992: 66–7).

This ambiguity is inherent in the film's structure. While the events and shape of the narrative are ostensibly dictated by a game of chance, as Smith points out, it is impossible for the film's own narrative to be truly random since Robbe-Grillet controls it. The author, moreover, readily accepted that this was so: 'I insist on control. I do not really want true aleatory narration' (ibid.: 67).

Whatever the means, it is of course the end result that matters most. Both *L'Eden et après* and *N. a pris les dés* are in so many ways products of the avant-garde cinema of a time dominated by experimentation with form in art. What makes these films extraordinary, however, is their structuring, musical in one case and mathematical in the other – structures of which most spectators would not be aware. In the absence of this awareness, the films come across as intriguing, certainly, yet confusing at times – a confusion arising from the attempt to shoehorn musical and mathematical structures into a largely visual medium. The film-maker and his characters may be playing games, in which the spectator is implicitly invited to participate, though not in the same way that the viewer of a murder is enjoined to solve the mystery. The films' titles both have a linguistic ambiguity that may point to the futility of such an approach: 'Eden and after' or 'Eden – so what?', and 'N took the dice' (but may not have thrown them). Like the modern art that inspires them, Robbe-Grillet's games have much less to do with the resolution of enigmas than with the intellectual and sensorial pleasures of spectatorial participation.

5 'But chance has its laws as well, they say'

Le Jeu avec le feu

In another parodic excursion into the detective genre, the plot of this 1975 film concerns the kidnapping of Claudia, 20-year-old daughter of a rich banker, Georges de Saxe, widower and father of a 22-year-old son, Jean. If the father alerts the police, the daughter will be burned alive and her body will never be found. In order to protect his daughter from this threat, de Saxe brings in a private detective who suggests putting her in a brothel for her safety. All is not what it seems, however, as, in spite of the existence of a ransom note signed by Claudia, the latter keeps reappearing at their home as if nothing had happened. Things are further complicated by de Saxe's incestuous desires for his daughter. Eventually, he decides to call in the police, but before he can finish dialling their number, there is an explosion and Claudia runs screaming from her room. It seems that, intending to burn papers in her fireplace, the young woman had inadvertently thrown an old celluloid doll onto the flames which had exploded, nearly causing a fire, and minor burns to Claudia. The threat of the hostage's execution by fire if the police were called appears to have been carried out, albeit symbolically. To calm his daughter's fears, Georges promises not to contact the police: 'Après tout', he says, 'tu n'as pas été enlevée, et tout cela ressemble à un jeu'.[6] De Saxe then entrusts Claudia to a couple of friends, Francis and Eva who go off on a journey. Meanwhile, he remains in contact with the unknown criminals who keep giving him instructions which he ignores. One after the other, all of the supposed kidnappers' threats appear to be carried out. Finally, in an obvious parody of the dénouement typical of the genre, all is revealed: Francis is none other than one of the criminals, Franck in disguise, while Claudia has been attempting to extort money from the bank to fund a revolutionary organisation of which she is a member, and de Saxe himself has been exploiting the opportunities created by the situation to satisfy his incestuous desires for his daughter.

As the above summary makes clear, the film reproduces many of Robbe-Grillet's favourite themes: once again purloining recognisable themes and topoi from the detective story, the film narrative takes us through a series of events which may or may not be happening, from the kidnapping of a young woman, her imprisonment in a brothel by sexual aggressors and eventual rape, to incestuous desires and the

6 'After all, you have not been kidnapped and the whole affair is like some sort of game'

commission of sacrilegious acts for the erotic satisfaction of the male kidnappers (in a mock wedding scene, the young bride is stripped and crucified for her sexual misdemeanours). The figure of the young witch as a dangerous sexual temptation is instantly recognisable from our acquaintance with *Glissements*, made the previous year (1974). In the enforced sexual education of a young woman, there are echoes here, too, of a wider erotic intertext, from Sade's *La Philosophie dans le boudoir* and *Justine* to the initially pseudonymous *Histoire d'O* and *L'Image*.[7] The doubling motif, beloved of Robbe-Grillet, finally, is an important structural element, as several characters in the film have aliases, and the principal protagonists, notably father and daughter, have villainous alter egos.

In addition to playing with these stereotypes from erotic literature, Robbe-Grillet again toys with the expectations of a spectator familiar with the crime genre, and uniquely here with the motif of fire as another commonplace of both erotic and religious iconography, motif and theme to which the film title ironically draws attention. Lefèvre outlines the dominant role of fire:

> Les flammes cernent une jeune suppliciée sur un vitrail ou transforment un inoffensif chat noir en animal maléfique. Une recette culinaire inédite utilise le feu pour la dégustation de la femme nue flambée au cognac. C'est aussi le feu qui sert au mécanisme d'une remise de rançon digne des Pieds Nickelés bricoleurs. Et si la musique de Verdi s'invite pour jouer avec le feu, c'est certainement pour le thème de l'enfant au bûcher du 'Trouvère'. Le feu se réserve aussi le dernier mot, avec une poursuite-épilogue filmée sur le mode burlesque. La voiture des méchants explose et devient une véritable boule de feu.[8] (2005: 21)

---

7 Pauline Réage, *Histoire d'o* (1954); Paris, Pauvert, 1975, and Jean(ne) de Berg, *L'Image*, Paris, Éditions de Minuit, 1956. Réage was eventually shown to be a pseudonym for Dominique Aury, and *L'Image* is now thought to have been written by Catherine Robbe-Grillet.

8 'Flames surround a young female victim on a stained-glass window or transform a harmless black cat into an evil beast. An unpublished cooking recipe uses fire for the enjoyment of a naked woman flambée in cognac. Fire also serves as the method employed to deliver a ransom, one worthy of the Pieds Nickelés. And if Verdi's music is de rigueur for a game with fire, it has to be the theme of the child burned at the stake in *Il Trovatore*. Fire also has the last word in the epilogue, where a car chase is filmed in burlesque mode. The villains' car explodes to become a veritable ball of fire.' (The *Pieds Nickelés* or 'Workshy' was the name of a French cartoon series by Louis Forton, first published in 1908, and *Il Trovatore* is the name of a grand opera by Verdi, first staged in 1857.)

The burning images are strongly intertextual within the Robbe-Grillet corpus, reminiscent of scenes in *L'Eden*, and especially in *Glissements*, to be made three years later, where fire will also function as a means of sacrifice and the punishment of innocent victims. At the same time, the recurrence across the films of such a powerful visual image suggests a personal authorial preoccupation with this ancient symbol of both destruction and purification on the one hand and sexual passion on the other – both recognisable Robbe-Grilletian themes in tension the one with the other.

Un bruit qui rend fou

Written by Robbe-Grillet and co-directed with Dimitri de Clercq, this film, dated 1995, raises once again the question of authorship posed by *Marienbad*. Like the two previous films, it is also a ludic exercise: 'D'essence ludique, *Un Bruit Qui Rend Fou* propose un divertisse-ment raffiné pour épicuriens exigeants dotés d'une intelligence des sens autant que curieux des constructions de l'esprit'[9] (Prédal 2005: 165). This quotation insists both on game-playing and on the elitism of an art that pleases at a high level. At another level, *Un bruit* is clearly a parody of the *film policier* and *film noir*. The narrative is punctuated by shots of a man holding a gun and shining his lamp, either into the depths of the ocean or onto some unknown figure – an obvious cliché from crime fiction. The familiar erotic themes of Robbe-Grillet's fictions are also present in scenes of sadomasochism and murder. In a café on the Greek isle of Hydra, inhabited mainly by poor fishermen, four Chinamen are playing mah-jong. While the four men are absorbed in their game, and talking softly, we distinctly hear a 'maddening noise' – the irritating sound made by the ivory dominos as they are slapped down in quick succession onto the lacquered table.

This scene is intercut with shots of a singing lesson, the activities of fishermen on their little boats, and the sudden appearance among them of a strange-looking ship with red sails and a dragon with fierce eyes painted on the prow. This alien craft transforms the little Greek port into one from the mythical Orient, and provides the catalyst for

9 'Essentially ludic, *A Maddening Noise* offers a refined entertainment to demanding epicureans equipped with both an intelligence of the senses and a curiosity about how the mind is constructed.'

a narrative that takes the spectator out of reality and into a landscape of dreams and the imaginary. An intradiegetic narrator named Gold dictates the script into a tape recorder as it is enacted, ostensibly a documentary about life on the Greek island, but the apparent realism of this scenario is quickly eroded by a superstitious rumour that a man named Franck is about to return. Every year, he arrives on the junk with the blood-red sails in search of his lost fiancée. This ghostly narrative strongly recalls the myth of the *Flying Dutchman*, a ghost ship that can never go home, doomed to sail the oceans forever, and it clearly conflicts in the film with a realism over which it is ultimately seen to triumph. This oneiric narrative is further complicated by the quest of a man named Nord for his daughter, locked away in a house of pleasure called the Blue Villa where she is known as Lotus-Flower. Nord's wife is said to have been murdered by revolutionaries. His daughter Sara, for whom he has an incestuous attraction, also dies. Was she too murdered, or did she commit suicide? The answer is supposed to be brought by the ghostly sailor. Meanwhile, in the 'real' world, police inspector Thieu records his own, more prosaic version of events which conflicts sharply with those of the fantasy. Against the leitmotif of the noise made by the dominoes, the ghost ship and its quest become inextricably confused with the narrator's fantasies and obsessions which in turn contrast with and eventually take the place of the inspector's realist account of events. In a final, dreamlike scene, the two lovers return from the grave to embark in their ghost ship on a final voyage into a timeless Far East.

Robbe-Grillet is obviously playing here with the *Flying Dutchman* legend, beloved of literature, music and painting, but at the same time, he is teasing the spectator with notions of realism and anti-realism. Like the mah-jong game that punctuates the film, the narrative presents itself as a game, an artistic exercise, filled with stimulating and pleasurable moments, and one that is not to be confused with reality.

The film was shot on the Island of Hydra in 1994, and the cinematography certainly captures the splendour of its natural surroundings with great success. For instance, a remarkably beautiful shot appears to combine the fantasy and eroticism of *The Flying Dutchman* myth and Millais's *The Death of Ophelia*. A pair of frightening eyes painted on the ship's prow designed to ward off evil bears down on the semi-naked body of a beautiful but lifeless young woman, floating in the sea, her violently torn dress, deathly pallor and supine position implying a tragic fate, perhaps at the hands of a male rapist. Is she real or the fantasy creation of one of the characters? The symmetry of the image centres on the ripples that fan out from the ship to engulf the corpse and are clearly unrealistic, since the ship is moving towards and not away from the woman. This movement of the water from ship to woman thus suggests waves of magical influence emanating from the hypnotic eyes, transparent symbol of the male voyeur. This ship reappears later, as it enters a Mediterranean port.[10]

As in *Trans-Europ-Express*, *Un bruit* comments self-reflexively on its own construction, including the use of a tape recorder to build the narrative scene by scene, shot by shot. The narrator, who may be guilty of murder and incest, and who is telling his own story in this manner, is cut off by the sudden arrival of the police commissioner which causes the man to commit suicide. Thus are both story and narrative brought to an abrupt and enigmatic end.

This film is another artistic game, an interesting yet narcissistic attempt to construct a detective story around well-known works of art and music – Richard Wagner's opera of 1843 being the best-known example of the latter – and the repetition of images that echo them. However, the film has other, arguably more appealing qualities. While the film title draws attention to the capacity of repeated sounds to irritate, visual repetition is seen to be aesthetically pleasing and intellectually stimulating. Ultimately, *Un bruit qui rend fou* succeeds as an intelligent parody of the thriller and above all as a succession of beautiful and culturally resonant tableaux.

Some concluding remarks

Bruce Morrissette poses the question of whether the predilection for games and game structures is evidence of excessive formalism in Robbe-Grillet's work. There is certainly to be observed a reaction against the *engagement* of an earlier generation of writers, such as Sartre and Camus. But, as Morrissette observes, 'game for Robbe-Grillet has come to mean structural freedom, absence of traditional rules of transition, viewpoint, chronology, and other parameters of

10 René Prédal evokes the oriental character of this boat which he calls a 'death ship' (2005: 168, fig. 3, 169, fig. 4 and 173).

previous fiction, and, on the constructive side, an invitation to create new models, to develop new combinations, to push ahead even further the aptly termed *nouveau roman*' (1966: 163).

However, these films are in one important respect a personal experiment in that they metaphorise the tension between creative freedom and control that inhabits Robbe-Grillet himself. So one might say that he plays at playing with chance. He also plays with his own presence and its influence in the films he creates:

> RS: You are something of a voyeuristic Cartesian in this film where the narrator says, 'Je regarde, donc je derobe'[*sic*] ('I look, therefore I conceal' or 'I look, therefore I rob').
>
> RG: (laughter) There was a pun using the homophone of '*dérobe*': *des robes* (dresses) – also, as I have often said about my other works, a pun on *dé-robe* (un-dress), which explains why there are so many naked young women, and on *dé-Robbe*, or removing Robbe-Grillet. (Fragola and Smith 1992: 68)

Above all, these brilliant exercises in style may be considered a manifesto for, as well as examples of 'ludic cinema'. The characters of these films play, and Robbe-Grillet himself plays with appearances, identities, ambiguities, time and space, eroticism, references to music and art. All the films discussed in this chapter may be said to embody an apparently infinite series of regressive mirror images, reflecting and, ironically, themselves constituting the very activity of playing.

Robbe-Grillet appears to reject the tyranny of an overall meaning imposed from above, and so we should not expect all enigmas to be finally resolved, including that of the tension between random creativity and authorial control. The very provision of unambiguous answers is parodied in the epilogue of *L'Eden* when the waiter puts all the pictures away as the students dream of their holidays. Lefèvre sums up the message, if message there is, of this final scene, and at the same time, captures the essential basis of Robbe-Grillet's 'cinéma ludique': 'Sordide trafic d'œuvres d'art ou retour sur une histoire qui n'a pas eu lieu? Une fois de plus la dictature du sens sombre dans le faux-semblant et l'ambiguïté'[11] (2005: 17).

---

11 'A sordid traffic in works of art or comment upon a story that has not taken place? The dictatorship of meaning sinks into ambiguity.'

References

Deleuze, Gilles (1989), *Cinema 2: The Time Image*, London, Athlone Press.

Fragola, Anthony N. and Smith, Roch C. (1992), *The Erotic Dream Machine: Interviews with Alain Robbe-Grillet on His Films*, Carbondale and Edwardsville, Southern Illinois University Press.

Gallet, Pascal-Emmanuelle (ed.) (1982), *Alain Robbe-Grillet: Œuvres Cinématographiques*, Édition vidéographique critique, Paris, Ministère des relations extérieures, Cellule d'animation culturelle.

Gardies, André (2005), 'Le travail du double', in Prédal, *Robbe-Grillet Cinéaste*, 105–43.

Klein, Melanie (1949), *The Psychoanalysis of Children*, 3rd edn, International Psychoanalytical Library, 22, London, Hogarth Press.

Kuhn, Ira (1976), 'Speculations about Games and Reality: Robbe-Grillet and Uwe Johnson', in Grant E. Kaiser (ed.), *Fiction, Form, Experience: The French Novel from Naturalism to the Present*, Montréal, Éditions France-Québec, 185–98.

Lefèvre, Raymond (2005), 'Neuf voyages aux pays des images mentales', in Prédal, *Robbe-Grillet Cinéaste*, 11–24.

Morrissette, Bruce (1966), 'Games and Game Structures in Robbe-Grillet', *French Studies* 41: 159–63.

Prédal, René (2005), 'Des images pour *Un bruit qui rend fou*', in *Robbe-Grillet Cinéaste*, Études publiées sous la direction de René Prédal, Caen, Presses universitaires de Caen, 163–74.

Robbe-Grillet, Alain (2005), *Préface à une vie d'écrivain*, Paris, France Culture, Éditions du Seuil.

Stoltzfus, Ben (1985), *Alain Robbe-Grillet: The Body of the Text*, London and Toronto, Associated University Presses.

Van Wert, William F. (1977), *The Film Career of Alain Robbe-Grillet*, London, George Prior Publishers.

Winnicott, D. (1971), *Playing and Reality*, London, Tavistock.

4

Beginnings and endings: orientalism and the erotic in *L'Immortelle* and *C'est Gradiva qui vous appelle*

Of the ten films directed by Robbe-Grillet, three of them have had oriental settings: Istanbul for *L'Immortelle*, Djerba for *L'Eden et après* and Marrakesh for *C'est Gradiva qui vous appelle*. This choice of location, to some degree motivated by financial considerations, also reflects a personal predilection to which Robbe-Grillet has himself confessed. However, his liking for such settings goes beyond mere personal preference and practical necessity. The Orient, on the face of it, represents a world of stereotypes: the mysterious, the exotic, the veiled or imprisoned female beauty, the ineluctably strange, as typified by those places of the East that haunt the Western imagination – the souk, the harem, the kasbah, windswept deserts of rippling white sands and marble-covered palaces and minarets. The figures that inhabit these locations are also the stuff of the imaginary: besabred riders on arab steeds, sinister figures in boutiques and alleyways, and above all, lovely young Caucasian women, usually blonde and blue-eyed, who disappear and reappear to the consternation and fascination of a hero who is, of course, a white Frenchman. The pretext for such settings, therefore, is the eroticism that for Robbe-Grillet pervades, not the real Orient but the Orient of myth.

Robbe-Grillet's rejection of any socio-political content for art has already been discussed in earlier chapters. Neither *Marienbad* nor *L'Immortelle*, both made during France's involvement in the Algerian war, contains any references to politics or society, for example. Yet, at other less explicit levels, *L'Immortelle*, *L'Eden et après* and *C'est Gradiva qui vous appelle* may be said to have political contents in a colonialist discourse that is evident at a number of levels. All three appear on the face of it to be post-colonial films that exhibit an ironic awareness of the stereotyping of the Orient, as Robbe-Grillet has himself made clear in interviews in relation to these films and to his novel, *La Jalousie*.[1]

The representations of the East in *L'Immortelle*, as in *L'Eden* and *Gradiva* are designed to challenge stereotype by exaggerating it. Yet, as in the art they are claimed to be critiquing, such representations, ironic or not, are inescapably erotic. One also senses an authorial fascination in the emphasis on strangeness and the preoccupation with other, both of which tend to undermine any parodic effects.

Focusing on the two films in which these effects are most pronounced, his first, *L'Immortelle* and his last, *C'est Gradiva qui vous appelle*, I shall interrogate the validity of Robbe-Grillet's claims, and of those critics who support them.

L'Immortelle

Around 1959 to 1960, the film producer, Samy Halfon approached Robbe-Grillet and asked if he would like to make a film. The latter expressed doubts about the popular success of any such project, given the small readership of his novels, but Halfon brushed aside such objections, insisting that the only thing that mattered was that the film be shot in Istanbul. It seemed that the latter had a large sum of Turkish money that could not be taken out of the country, and that he therefore needed to spend in Turkey. When the film was made and exported outside Turkey, the problem would be solved. Robbe-Grillet and his wife, Catherine left immediately for Istanbul, where he wrote the script. Before shooting could begin, however, a bloody revolution in Turkey obliged Robbe-Grillet to leave the country and put the project on hold. It was during this period of waiting to return to Istanbul that he was approached by another producer, asking if he would like to write a script for Resnais, and that *Marienbad* was conceived. The completion of the *Marienbad* script happily coincided with a restoration of order in Turkey, and Robbe-Grillet and Catherine were able to return to Istanbul to commence shooting *L'Immortelle* (2005: 197–205).

The original title of the film was *Les chiens* ('The Dogs'), but this title had to be changed for reasons of religious and political sensitivity

---

1 Robbe-Grillet's own colonial experiences as an agronomist in the Caribbean were reflected in *La Jalousie*.

(ibid.: 200). Robbe-Grillet was perfectly happy to comply with this condition, particularly as he had a sentimental attachment to Turkey's capital city, having met his wife, Catherine, there ten years earlier.

L'Immortelle was therefore the first film that Robbe-Grillet both scripted and directed, and as such, proved to be in part very much a learning process. The film appeared in 1963, eighteen months after *Marienbad*. Critical reception was almost unanimously hostile, and Robbe-Grillet has said that it is the least satisfactory of all his films (ibid.: 211), and has repeatedly regretted the fact that the former film suffered from comparison with the latter, since they were different in every respect. He conceded that the stiffness of the acting prevented the film from being a commercial success, and that critics were shocked that the leading actor did not seem to move normally, that he did not seem to be able to touch the lead actress, as if he were not really in the same world as she was (Fragola and Smith 1992: 7–8, 27). Nevertheless, in 1963, the film was awarded the prix Delluc, at the time the most prestigious French prize awarded to a film director, and a prize which recognized the place of the film in an already esteemed tradition of the marriage of the popular and intellectual traditions in French cinema.[2]

Everything in the film is seen implicitly through the eyes of the Frenchman, a certain Professor N who arrives in Istanbul, and whose vision of the city is influenced by stereotyped fantasies of the Orient, gleaned from postcards and popular novels. He meets a mysterious young woman who calls herself Lale, and with whom he visits the city, including the Selim Mosque, a belly-dancing club, bazaars and what appears to be an ancient graveyard. Lale tells the man that 'all of this is false' and 'for the tourists' – 'Vous voyez que ce n'est pas une vraie ville', Lale tells N, 'C'est un décor opérette pour une histoire d'amour'.[3] Indeed, as the narrative progresses, it becomes increasingly clear that the spectator cannot rely on any information it provides. The woman speaks Turkish but she is clearly French, and it is suggested later that her name is not Lale but Lucie. 'Lale' suddenly disappears, and N spends the rest of the film searching for her, revis-

2 The 'prix Delluc' was founded in 1937 in homage to Louis Delluc, the first French journalist to write about the cinema and founder of the *cinéclubs*, or local film societies. The prize is awarded to auteur films judged to combine artistic merit and public appeal.

3 'You can see that it is not a real city. It's an operetta set for a love story.'

iting the places she had taken him. The search culminates in her death (which may or may not be accidental, and indeed may or may not have happened) at the wheel of a car. The crash may have been deliberately caused by a sinister male figure with two vicious-looking hounds, but his presence at the scene may be purely circumstantial. This scene is repeated obsessively from different angles and perhaps points of view, as if in a desperate yet futile attempt to discover what really happened. In a final series of shots, it is the man and not the woman who is seen dead at the wheel, and the film cuts to the woman laughing, but again, there is no guarantee that this version is more reliable than any other. Thus, like all of Robbe-Grillet's anti-realist narratives, the viewer is positioned as a detective doomed to failure. Like the slats of the blind through which N and the spectator gaze at the beginning and end of the film, Robbe-Grillet's narrative is ultimately as impenetrable as the city of Istanbul itself.[4]

Unsurprisingly, therefore, as Robbe-Grillet himself suggests, the Istanbul of *L'Immortelle* is not the real Istanbul but a product of the imaginary and a function of the narrative generated by it: 'This hero is a Frenchman who arrives in Turkey and already has conjured up fantasies about the Orient – picture postcards or memories of novels that he has read, such as those of Pierre Loti, with sequestered harems, etc. What he sees is obviously heavily influenced by stereotypes of Istanbul and the Orient' (Fragola and Smith 1992: 27).[5] Edward Saïd identifies our stereotyped notions of the East as a place of both familiarity and otherness, of exoticism and eroticism: 'The Orient at large [...] vacillates between the West's contempt for what is familiar and its shivers of delight in – or fear of – novelty' (2003: 59). If we believe the author, such contents are to be read in an ironic and parodic perspective, according to which it is precisely this stereotypical view of the Orient that is interrogated.

Robbe-Grillet defines *L'Immortelle* as a film about nothing, about 'le *vrai*, le *faux* et le *faire-croire* [qui] se développe en tant que réflexion

---

4 The blind inescapably recalls Robbe-Grillet's 1957 novel, *La Jalousie*, the title of which has two possible meanings: 'jealousy' and a shutter through which a jealous man may watch his wife, and whose perception of events may thus be obscured and distorted by this partial view. In the multiple versions of Lale's death, there are also unmistakeable echoes of the repeated car-crash scenes in *La Jalousie*.

5 We note the similar terms in which the author talks about *L'Eden et après*: 'Tunisia is merely a Tunisia of postcards [...] stereotypes of our charming society [...] Club Med, etc.' (Fragola and Smith 1992: 61).

sur la réalité (ou le *peu de réalité* comme on voudra)'[6] (Robbe-Grillet 1963a: 129), but the film does have identifiable referents in the representation of women in colonialist art. As Noël Burch puts it, 'Il s'agit de récréer après Ingres, Nerval, et toute une littérature/peinture du xix siècle français, un réseau d'équivalences entre deux entités également mystérieuses et menaçantes, la Femme et l'Orient. Ce qui, dans le système de l'auteur, où l'art n'a que mépris pour les "idéologies", n'est qu'un vaste stéréotype "lavé", un de plus'[7] (2005: 28).

The Istanbul presented to us from the outset is a colonial one. The film begins with a commentary spoken in a feminine voice, described in the *cinéroman* as 'profonde et sensuelle'[8] (Robbe-Grillet 1963b), itself a stereotype of what for Saïd is in the Western imagination the 'supine, feminine Orient' (2003: 220). This voice-over accompanies travelling shots of the shores of the Bosporus, which are lined with the ruins of old Constantinople, all of which comes across as a documentary of the period on the colonial past. As in so many films and documentaries, Robbe-Grillet's Orient is like a living museum, where the natives rarely make an appearance, and even when they do, they appear idle. The film consciously exhibits the Orient as steeped in an erotic languor recognisable from the paintings of Ingres and Delacroix. Work is not part of this 'fairy-tale' world: 'Seul dans ce film en effet le personnage d'intellectuel blanc français "travaille"'[9] (Burch 2005: 30), and as the agent of the quest for the woman, he is the conscious subject of the diegesis (N, therefore, perhaps standing for 'Narrator', as Stoltzfus suggests: 'The film's diegesis evolves inside N's mind' (1985: 108)).

The proverbial cruelty of the Orient is suggested by shots of the man with the dogs and by allusions to stories of sequestered women made by the enigmatic Catherine Sarayan, played by Catherine Robbe-Grillet. Women are depicted in the narrative as deeply ambivalent. On the one hand, essentially submissive, another powerful and persistent

---

6 'the real, the false and the make-believe [which] develop as a reflection on reality (or the lack of reality if you prefer)'

7 'The aim was to recreate in the manner of Ingres, Nerval and an entire literary and artistic tradition of the French nineteenth century a network of equivalences between two equally mysterious and threatening entities, Woman and the Orient, a project which, from the author's point of view, according to which art has nothing but contempt for ideologies, is just one more "sanitised" stereotype'

8 'deep and sensual'

9 'The only character who works in the film is actually a white French intellectual'

cliché of the Orient, they are indolent creatures kept by men. They spend their time gazing at the Bosporus and give enigmatic answers to the male protagonist's questions. The elusive and mysterious woman who persistently eludes the white French male hero, has all the airs of a nervous and ultimately submissive harem concubine. The cliché of the oriental woman's inferiority to men is emphasised in the mosque where only men may pray. As the architect of the Fall, Eve's descendants are also as dangerous as they are inferior. In a lengthy scene, in which a scantily clad belly-dancer with snake-like arms gyrates hypnotically before an audience of men, like the mythical siren luring them to their doom, women's sexuality is linked to the menacingly strange, a motif returned to again and again in the portrayal of the female lead, the teasingly seductive Lale, shots of whom repeatedly link her to death: a passing funeral cortège, an ancient cemetery and, finally, herself as corpse or corpse like. Creature of mystery and ambivalence, woman in this perspective is both desired and feared.

Such images are stereotypes presented as stereotypes, as a self-aware and therefore self-critical racism, and yet there is meaning in these images. In spite of their apparent parodic self-awareness, the colonialist attitudes persist. In view of his own sexual proclivities, Robbe-Grillet's claims to stand outside the erotic objectification of the oriental woman must be disingenuous to some degree.

A worrying strangeness

L'Immortelle, or *The Immortal One* is an ambiguous title that refers as much to the mysterious woman who is at the centre of the narrative as to the city of Istanbul in which the film is set. This ambivalent title sets the tone for a film that can be read on a number of different but related levels: exploration of the concept and nature of reality, of that sense of the uncanny associated with scenes and locations that appear at once familiar and strange, of the fetishistic and sadomasochistic elements in male–female sexuality, of the mythic nature of man's perceptions and representations of the feminine.

There is in Freud's notion of the uncanny a tension between the familiar and the strange that is identifiable in all of Robbe-Grillet's films, but particularly so in *L'Immortelle*. In the very concept of the uncanny, we find both Robbe-Grillet's artistic conception of reality, and his relation to sexuality as fetishistic, that is, defined by castration anxiety and ambivalence towards the feminine which is perceived as both an object of desire and a reminder of the threat of castration – a body at once strange and yet oddly familiar:

> The fetish is a substitute for the woman's (the mother's) penis that the little boy once believed in and – for reasons once familiar to us – does not want to give up [...] [The fetish] remains a token of triumph over the threat of castration and a protection against it. It also saves the fetishist from becoming a homosexual, by endowing women with the characteristic which makes them tolerable as sexual objects. (Freud 1984a [1920]: 352–4)[10]

The French term for the Freudian uncanny, *l'inquiétante étrangeté*, or 'worrying strangeness', more effectively conveys the disturbing nature of the feelings and sensations associated with it. This 'strangeness' infects the general location of Istanbul, where the male hero obsessively returns to sites in the ancient Turkish city in search of a mysterious and beautiful woman who continually appears and disappears, a woman who may or may not be real or alive, even if she once was.[11] It also pervades every aspect of the film narrative: characters, images, locations, dialogue, sound and music, and chronology.[12]

This uncanny atmosphere is partly generated by the film's fairy-tale structure. The Eastern location, Istanbul, is itself redolent of the fairy-tale and pantomime genres (see below) which favour orientalism and the exotic – of which *The Arabian Nights* and *Aladdin* are probably the best-known examples.

The film's themes of questing, loss and death, and the eroticism that surrounds them, are as old as storytelling itself. Like many fairy tales, *L'Immortelle* is at its most basic level about the male quest for woman. This quest is the most ancient of narrative forms, *Sleeping Beauty*, *Snow White*, *Beauty and the Beast* and *Cinderella* being relatively recent and enduring models. Bewitched by the beauty of a mysterious woman, with whom he has spent a few moments only, N.

---

10 The fetishistic character of the erotic in Robbe-Grillet's films will be discussed in more detail in Chapters 5 and 6.

11 See Freud 1985a (1919). For a detailed discussion of Freud's notion of the uncanny in relation to *L'Année dernière à Marienbad*, see Chapter 1.

12 Old places like Istanbul suggest the ghosts of the past, a motif typical of nearly all Robbe-Grillet's films in which there is frequently an eruption of the past in the present. It can be no coincidence that a retrospective on Robbe-Grillet is entitled 'Une Étrange Familiarité', or 'A Strange Familiarity' (Gallet 1982: 12–19).

obsessively visits each of the locations in which the woman has been present but without success. As in the *Cinderella* fairy tale, each of the characters he meets gives a different account of her identity (in this case, her appearance, name, nationality, etc.).

A 'fairy-tale' unreality also informs the role of objects and scenarios in the film, which are not interpretable on a realist, but on an aesthetic and structural level. The 'ancient' statuette in a gift shop which is later revealed to be a replaceable copy seems to function as a *mise en abyme* of the self-conscious fakeness that permeates the film narrative, as reflected in the statue-like postures of the secondary characters, whose remoteness from any identifiable reality situates them as mere copies of real people. Dogs, a diary fragment, boats, chairs, all of these objects which appear throughout the narrative in aleatory fashion are uncanny in both their inexplicability in realist terms and their suggestive insistence. The aim seems to be to get beyond their representational function, emptying them of symbolic meaning in order to reverse what Slavoj Žižek calls 'the dematerialisation of the real', replacing it with a fantasised, psychological real (2002: 13–14). As Robbe-Grillet himself avers, 'le réel, c'est le moment où le monde semble perdre son sens'.[13]

Repetition further undermines any attempt to construct a conventional linear narrative. Scenes are repeated with slight variations. Furthermore, the very themes of questing, of loss and death that run through the narrative are themselves essentially repetitive. Loss and death are eternal elements of the human condition, while the quest for woman is represented as never-ending, unfulfilled. From a psychoanalytic point of view, one might say that the male quest in both film and fairy tale, and indeed in all narratives constructed on this model, enact the *Spaltung*, or gap, between need and demand, between happiness and the satisfaction of desire. This fairy-tale framework and its uncanny resonances are clearly linked to Robbe-Grillet's rejection of realism and his conception of the real as psychological.[14]

The film narrative is punctuated by Turkish songs and dialogue which add to the sense of estrangement for the European spectator.

13 'The real is the moment when the world seems to lose its meaning'. See Chapter 1 for discussion of the distinction between the real and realism.
14 In the quest for a woman who appears and disappears and finally dies, this film has clear similarities at a basic structural level to Hitchcock's *Vertigo* (1958) and may have been inspired by it.

First impressions suggest that such elements are nothing more than stereotype, whose function is to operate self-consciously as such. However, the songs in particular appear, on closer inspection, to have more complex functions. Some of the spoken Turkish is repeated in summarised form in French, but the greater part remains untranslated and none of the many songs is translated. There is a ludic element at play here in a kind of 'Fort! Da!' game, since the Turkish lyrics of the songs, which may be said simultaneously to conceal and reveal, are directly relevant to the themes of the narrative: a quest for the lost object of desire, the immortality of beauty in women and in objects, sadomasochistic pain, death and necrophilia.[15]

Echoing the film's title, the opening song unites woman and city: the latter is beautiful because it is where the man has seen his elusive love. This ambiguity is thus reinforced here, and repeated at the end of the film: 'I've seen lots of countries, no place is more beautiful than here.' Again, the woman and the city are metonymically associated. All the songs are traditional Turkish love songs, expressing mourning for infidelity and loss: 'Your image becomes like an oasis. What if I can't see you again? I don't understand why lovers are dying. Do they also long for someone like me?' These lyrics, typical of all the songs in the film, repeatedly and stereotypically express longing, loss, love and death. Much of it is Sufi music often heard at Turkish funerals, and the closing song again focuses on absence and longing: 'You are my happiness, my soul. What will happen if I see you again?'

Female masochism, highlighted in all of the songs, in which a woman laments her suffering at the hands of a man who has abandoned her, is an especially dominant theme of the film, echoed in references to the shutting away of women in the mosque and their complicity in this condition and to an apparent willingness to be beaten. The heroine has clear masochistic tendencies. When the male hero teasingly threatens to beat her, she murmurs 'Oh, oui!' and runs off laughing. As Burch points out, this playful 'kiss chase' leads to the only 'living' sex of the film, all other sexual activity being of a necrophilic kind. For example, in a later shot, the man passes his hand across the face of the prostrate, lifeless woman, as if to close the eyes of a corpse (Burch 2005: 31–2).[16]

In addition to the thematic relevance of the lyrics, the melancholy

15 On necrophilia, see Freud 1984b (1920).
16 Chapter 6 develops the theme of necrophilia in greater depth.

music too is both familiar and strange. Sufi hymns to accompany 'death' rituals, for example, may be identified by those who know about such music, but even those who do not may recognise in their melancholy strains the expression of feelings of sadness, sensuality, longing and desire that these hymns convey.

The Turkish dialogue varies between the banal – the opening conversation between the fisherman and old woman, for example, is mundane but humorous, concerning empty chairs facing the harbour – and the esoteric when the old woman suddenly and uncharacteristically turns to literary questions: 'Do you know the poems of the Sultan Selim?' The themes of these poems are richness of empire and courtly love, associated with the 'Tulip' period of the Ottoman empire – themes with which the mysterious woman is directly and playfully associated by her name, Lale, which, she tells the professor, means 'tulip'. Like the songs, the mention of these poems by an apparently uneducated Turkish woman thus contributes to an overall sense of the uncanny, at least for those who understand Turkish, but even for those who do not, the inclusion of dialogue in a foreign language without subtitles is both perplexing and unsettling for the francophone let alone the anglophone spectator.

In leaving the Turkish of the songs and dialogue untranslated, Robbe-Grillet may in part be pointing to issues of representation across languages, and the impossibility of reality in all its fullness, while at the same time underlining the otherness that inevitably accompanies all forms of representation. The appearance in one scene of a young boy, speaking Greek and without translation, contributes to this effect. Jacques Derrida's notion of *Darstellung* as simply 'putting there' explains well the *L'Immortelle* case[17] (see Wolfreys 2007: 111).

Burch is right to see the film as not simply a rejection of cinematic realism, but as a flight from the real, from the growing unrest in the Islamic Orient, especially Algeria (2005: 33). Robbe-Grillet's Orient is one of erotic fantasy, and yet, at the same time, a metaphor for repressed male anxieties with regard to an increasingly liberated female condition. However, another kind of reality pervades this film at the level of the audial imagery we have been discussing. The notion of the uncanny that informs the film at all levels strongly suggests that the stereotype of the 'mysterious and magical and dangerous Orient'

17 I should like to express my gratitude to Özlem Galip and Ayşegül Balci for their help in translating the Turkish elements in this film.

is not merely readable at a parodic level. *L'Immortelle* represents an uncanny linked to woman as bait, as an image of beauty in death, associated with images of castration (dogs), and assuaged by fetishes (sadomasochism, necrophilia, an erotic focus on clothing and on parts of the female body). In other words, the imagery of the film is shot through with an authorial eroticism that inevitably casts Orient and Orientals in supporting roles in Robbe-Grillet's own theatre of sex, in which a white Western man plays the lead. At the same time, such images are subtle enough to retain an ambivalence that is artistically interesting. It is, of course, arguable that any greater explicitness of the kind associated with Robbe-Grillet's later films would have hindered the film's distribution at the time of its release.

C'est Gradiva qui vous appelle

Robbe-Grillet's last film, *C'est Gradiva qui vous appelle* (2006), is explicitly erotic in ways in which his first, *L'Immortelle* could not have been, but in so many other respects, it contains identical themes and preoccupations: sadomasochism, loss, a man's quest for a mysterious woman who appears and disappears.

In an uncanny mirroring of the mixed reception accorded to *L'Immortelle*, *Gradiva* achieved a measure of critical success at the Venice Film Festival in 2006, which has not been reflected in its wider critical reception.[18] Also echoing *L'Immortelle*'s parodic tendencies, the film exhibits features more generally associated with popular than with high culture. There are elements of Gothic-style melodrama and intertextual references to the short story, *Gradiva*, published by the Danish author, Wilhelm Jensen in 1903 which its author described as a 'Pompeian phantasy'. The story became famous as the subject of Freud's essay, 'Delusions and Dreams in Jensen's *Gradiva*' (1985b [1907]). Jensen's novella recounts the experiences of an archaeologist who, during a visit to Pompei, uncovers a bas-relief (piece of shallow carving or sculpture on background) representing a young woman. The carving shows her walking with her foot perpendicular to the ground, a detail which Freud reads in terms of an unconscious fetishism. The story relates how the archaeologist falls in love with this feminine figure, as he imagines seeing her at every street corner.

18 Sélection officielle hors compétition, Festival de Venise 2006.

Other cultural influences in the film derive from the eroticisation of the Orient, found in the work of early nineteenth-century French artists such as Eugène Delacroix, in particular, in the painting *The Death of Sardanapalus* (1827). This latter image acts as an important generator of plot and theme. All of these intertextual elements function partly at the level of anti-realism and parody, but, as in *L'Immortelle*, they also mesh with an intensely personal erotic dimension.

Robbe-Grillet himself provides a summary of his film which is worth quoting in full, as it provides some clues as to how the author intended his film to be read:

> A young English art critic, John Locke, is a lover of orientalist painting, and has a particular interest in the theme of the objectified woman: object in art, erotic object, object of a man's passion, and consequently, in the young slave-girl who is cruelly punished for pleasure, and in the inaccessible goddess that men dare not approach.
>
> He has just moved into a ruined palace in the Atlas mountains in Morocco, following in the footsteps of Delacroix, who is both the subject of a study he is engaged in and the focus of his sexual fantasies.[19]
>
> A man who pretends to be blind leads him into the clutches of a forger, Anatoli, who runs a secret nightclub behind the scenes where orientalist scenarios of a sadistic nature are enacted. Under the pretext of obtaining for him genuine sketches made by Delacroix in Morocco, Anatoli lures John into a trap so as to frame him for a sex crime committed by someone else.
>
> Among the pretty young women who take part in these scenarios is Claudine, Anatoli's new mistress. It is she who will serve as bait. Above all, however, it is Hermione's fleeting, enigmatic and ambivalent presence that haunts him throughout the film. Is she a ghost, victim of some conspiracy, or is she the mastermind behind all the events of the film?
>
> What John seems unaware of is that his pretty young servant, Belkis, with whom he spends his nights in sensual pleasures that are obviously reciprocated, is secretly in love with him. Lost in his own dreamworld,

19 In 1832, Eugène Delacroix had travelled to Africa with the comte de Mornay at the request of the Sultan of Morrocco. Inspired by the light and colours of the Moroccan landscape, he spent six months there, during which he produced eight notebooks of sketches to be developed later in his studio. These works, of great importance in the history of art, would be considered the beginnings of the movement later to be known as 'Orientalism' (Robbe-Grillet in *Gradiva* publicity pamphlet, Zootrope Films 2006).

John loves Belkis without knowing he does, totally oblivious that he is driving her toward a tragic end. (Zootrope Films 2006)

The tragic end in question is a 'Madame Butterfly-style' suicide, to accompany which Robbe-Grillet specifies the use of appropriate extracts from the Puccini opera (Robbe-Grillet 2002: 154).

In *Gradiva*, as in his previous films, young women frequently appear naked as the objects of sexual attention and violence by men. The image of the dead woman, 'son beau corps laiteux transpercé à coups de poignard'[20] (ibid.: 46), is a recurrent leitmotif, as is the sight of the blade of a knife about to be thrust into a female breast or groin. In the *cinéroman*, phrases such as 'le joli corps martyrisé'[21] (ibid.: 83) suggest a certain authorial relish, in spite of an insistence on Robbe-Grillet's part that such imagery is not intended to be realist, but merely to infect the fevered imagination of a fictional character: 'Précisons bien que toute la séquence doit être ouvertement une scène de cauchemar, où le réalisme et le vraisemblable ne sont pas convoqués'[22] (ibid.: 84). Nevertheless, intertextual echoes of erotic moments from other works by Robbe-Grillet, both cinematic and novelistic, reinforce the sense of a controlling authorial presence that takes pleasure in the depiction of pain caused to beautiful young women, albeit in an unreal or imaginary world. The 'Triangle d'or' ('Golden Triangle') nightclub in which the murder of girls is ostensibly enacted, for example, directly refers us to his novel, *Souvenirs du Triangle d'or* ('Memories of the Golden Triangle', 1978), in which similar activities are carried out. The topos of the secret, labyrinthine mansion or chateau, honeycombed with dark corridors, off which nameless horrors occur not only has sadomasochistic associations but is also a classic horror-movie scenario, and in this case is directly inspired by an orientalist painting:

John se retrouve [...] dans un long couloir obscur où brillent à intervalles réguliers de faibles lumignons (simples bougies ou lampes à huile). S'éclairant mal avec la petite pile de poche [...] il ouvre une porte latérale à tâtons et trouve un interrupteur électrique. La lumière qu'il déclenche [...] laisse voir une petite salle aux murs de pierre, arabo-médiévale, et un amas de chairs nues sanguinolentes: trois ou

20 'her beautiful milky body pierced by dagger blows'
21 'the pretty martyred body'
22 'It should be clear that the entire sequence is obviously a nightmare in which realism and believability are not the aim'

quatre filles exécutées à coups de poignard [...] La composition rappelle beaucoup le tableau orientaliste intitulé «La justice du chérif» de Benjamin Constant.[23] (Ibid.: 107–8)

The *Gradiva* motif, with its erotic and fetishistic associations, is itself not new in Robbe-Grillet's work, as Raylene Ramsay observes when she makes indirect links between Jensen's tale, volcanic imagery in one of the novels, and sadomasochistic treatment of young females. Her observation, contained in her 1992 book, pre-dates the *cinéroman* by ten and the film itself by fourteen years:

> Vesuvius, part of the play of the recursive V in *Topologie d'une cité fantôme*, intertextual borrowing from Jensen's *Gradiva* [...] is conventionally a metaphor of eruption of hidden violence and apocalypse. In Robbe-Grillet's text, this ready-made generator is part of a proliferating series of elements that evoke the violation of the immobilized female body (young and beautiful for eternity) and death. Yet the volcano and the rocks it spews forth to wound vulnerable young females, however doll-like and unreal, is also clearly and ironically individuated, a self-conscious metaphor not only of the inner violence of the text but also of the pain/pleasure of a personal psychosexual sadistic drive. (Ramsay 1992: 70)

Ramsay's reading of the *Gradiva* borrowing in *Topologie* is equally applicable to the later film.

Orientalism

Unlike *L'Immortelle*, *Gradiva*, as we saw above, contains direct references to orientalist art. Like the Gothic, orientalism in art and literature dates back to the late eighteenth century, and was especially fashionable in England and France. As John Berger argues, orientalist paintings by artists such as Delacroix and Ingres, which put the female body on view for the male spectator to enjoy, are also, in a sense, the popular 'soft-core' of their time, offering the wealthy the

23 'John finds himself [...] in a long, dark corridor lit at regular intervals by dim lamps (candles or oil lamps). Lighting his way with difficulty with the aid of a small torch [...] he gropingly opens a side door and finds a light switch. This reveals a small, stone-walled room of medieval-arab style, containing a mass of naked and bleeding bodies: three or four girls killed by dagger blows [...] The scene is strongly reminiscent of the orientalist painting entitled *The Sheik's Sentence* by Benjamin Constant.'

eighteenth-century equivalent of *Playboy* images to gaze upon in the privacy of their mansions and chateaux (1985: 85).

Edward Saïd sets the context, relating the popular status of orientalism as an eighteenth-century vogue to 'the interest taken in Gothic tales, pseudomedieval idylls, visions of barbaric splendour and cruelty [...] Later in the nineteenth century, in the works of Delacroix and literally dozens of other French and British painters, the oriental genre tableau carried representation into visual expression and a life of its own' (2003: 118). As Saïd argues, 'the Orient was viewed as something inviting French interest, penetration, insemination' (ibid.: 219). Saïd's use of language makes the point: the Orient was both an inferior and an erotic object, a feminine space for the West to rape, just as the harem was such a space in microcosm.

The location for *Gradiva* is Marrakesh. As in *L'Immortelle*, the characters have no psychological depth, the situations are purely schematic, and the landscape settings are chosen for their clichéd character as stereotypes of the Middle East. René Prédal comments: 'c'est le cadre rassurant du déjà vu, de la convention littéraire ou cinématographique que l'on va ensuite pervertir en donnant brusquement à chaque détail un sens inhabituel'[24] (2005: 148).

Much of the related imagery consists of sexist and racist stereotypes, which seem to contribute to the erotic objectification of young women. Indeed, Robbe-Grillet's own statements at times appear to privilege eroticism over art (Ramsay 1992: 252). In the publicity pamphlet produced by the film's distributors, for example, he emphasises the eroticism and male violence against women that is so often the subject of orientalist painting:

> Je pense que toute forme d'art a un rapport très fort avec l'Eros, mais, le plus souvent, il est complètement masqué. Il est ardu de trouver de l'eros [*sic*] dans une peinture de Mondrian. La peinture orientaliste a cela de particulier que tout est assumé, exhibé, au contraire. Il ne s'agit pas de décrire l'orient réel, mais plutôt le mythe de l'orient et celui-ci est principalement érotique: la femme enfermée, la femme victime, la femme esclave.[25] (Zootrope Films 2006)

24 'This is the reassuring framework of the already seen, of a literary or cinematic convention which will subsequently be perverted by suddenly endowing every detail with an unusual meaning.'

25 'I believe that all forms of art have a very strong relationship with Eros but that it is most often completely hidden. It is hard to find Eros in one of Mondrian's paintings. Orientalist painting is unusual in that, on the contrary, everything is

Robbe-Grillet's intertextual exploitation of Delacroix in particular and of orientalism in general is, then, not merely parodic. Here, the author more clearly than ever before, perhaps, identifies his interest in both the Orient and orientalism as an overridingly erotic one. What else do we learn from this statement? That the eroticism he favours is of a sadomasochistic nature, and that his films are 'auteur' films in both the positive and negative sense, that is, the personal erotic focus gives them a strong artistic coherence, but this focus can have reductive consequences. The question, therefore, is whether this mix, while keeping in touch with a popular filmic tradition, can produce cinematic art that both engages the senses and challenges the intellect.

Like the *Gradiva* and 'Vesuvius' motifs, the orientalist painter, Eugène Delacroix, is a primary generator of sadomasochistic eroticism in the film. There are specific references to Delacroix in an erotic context: John, Anatoli and Claudine view paintings by and read books on Delacroix in a number of scenes.[26] Delacroix's sadomasochism is well documented. For James H. Rubin, Delacroix was especially curious about Arab women's submissive acceptance of sexual domination (2001: 36). It is certainly the case that during his trip to Morocco of 1832, Delacroix did make numerous sketches of Arab scenes, including women. Like Robbe-Grillet, moreover, Delacroix directly linked sadomasochism to creativity which he saw as an erotic act: 'Delacroix [...] redefined the studio as a private site for the sexual domination of women' (Grigsby 2001: 71). He repeatedly had sex with his models, but he also conflated heterosexual intercourse and the act of painting. Delacroix's painting, *Death of Sardanapalus* (salon of 1827–28) which is specifically referred to in the film, and has a thematic as well as diegetic status in it, combines imagery of a fantastic Orient with melodrama and sadomasochistic violence against naked young women (ibid.: 72).

Rubin identifies the mythical and literary context: 'The composition shows an ancient Assyrian king, his palace at Nineveh besieged by rebels, taking his harem mistresses and possessions within [sic] him as he goes down in self-inflicted flame and slaughter' (ibid.: 33).[27]

---

recognised and exhibited. The aim is not to describe the real Orient but rather the mythical Orient which is fundamentally erotic, with women depicted as captives, victims, slaves.'

26 See Robbe-Grillet 2002: 10, 12, 13, 24, 27, 38, 41.

27 The inspiration for the painting was initially Byron's play of 1821, in which a harem's treasures are destroyed to avoid losing them to an enemy (Rubin 2001: 26–47).

Raylene Ramsay identified the erotic charge that this painting carried for Robbe-Grillet long before the film was made. In a short text by Robbe-Grillet, entitled 'Pour Sibylle Ruppert', written to accompany that artist's work, 'Dessins pour Lautréamont', she argues:

> the obsessive nightmare phantasies of death, cruelty, and the vulnerability of the body reappear. Robbe-Grillet speaks here of 'a great number of disembowelled horses [...] also with naked women splendidly full-formed mixed up in the carnage. I think of *The Death of Sardanapale*, evidently, but the scene that surrounds me would be situated a few minutes after the fragile instant immobilized by Delacroix in which all the curves of desire are still ranged in their day-time places. While here [...] what are offered to the senses in revulsion are the secret shames of the anatomy: the orifices torn open, the entrails spilling out, the secretions, the waste products.' (quoted by Ramsay 1992: 199–200; her translation)

Robbe-Grillet, and Ramsay after him, go on to link 'the sharp steel point' and 'the soft ignominious flesh'.

In an early scene in *Gradiva*, John Locke is leafing through a series of projected images, many of Delacroix, some depicting horses. John dwells longer on each, as the images increasingly take on an erotic character, culminating in a reproduction of *Death of Sardanapalus* (Robbe-Grillet 2002: 11–12). In a scene that follows, in which John and his servant Belkis are lying in bed evidently following a bout of love-making, the young woman lies on her front, with her arms around her head, and her naked back and buttocks clearly visible. In the *cinéroman*, Robbe-Grillet makes a specific link between Belkis's posture and that of the beautiful young mistress of the Sultan in Delacroix's painting: 'sa posture reproduit le plus possible celle de la femme allongée sur le lit du Sultan, dans le Sardanapale de Delacroix'[28] (ibid.: 16–17). Thus, the eroticisation of the Orient in orientalist painting is directly brought to life again here, but as in many of the film's other erotic scenes, without any clear parodic intent.

Fetishism, finally, has a central importance in Jensen's story, in Freud's reading of it, and in this painting. Discussing *Death of Sardanapalus*, Petra ten-Doesschate Chu (2001: 103) draws attention to the foot of a kneeling male figure in the foreground on the right. The foot describes a right angle and may have inspired Robbe-Grillet. Despite

28 'her posture reproduces as much as possible that of the woman lying on the sultan's bed in *Sardanapalus* by Delacroix'

being a male foot, it has the female characteristic of daintiness, and is clad in a slender, ornate slipper. The very name, Gradiva, as we have seen, means the walking woman, and we note that in Freud's analysis of Jensen's tale, her perpendicular foot has the phallic associations shared by all fetish objects.

Concluding remarks

Robbe-Grillet's use of erotic imagery in the context of Gothic and orientalist works is complex: ironic to some unmeasurable degree but equally, and perhaps more obviously visceral (the two are not necessarily incompatible). The use of this imagery certainly appears at times to be self-reflexively objectifying, but also celebratory of the female body, as indeed were the paintings that it inspired.

Paul Joannides notes the influence of Rubens in Delacroix's painting, positing a tension between beauty and its destruction as an inherent theme of the painting, tension that we might equally see in *Gradiva*:

> It has often been noted that perhaps the most beautiful figure in the painting, the woman in the right foreground – and it is the destruction of beauty that gives the painting its particularly distressing edge – is taken from one of the daughters of Leucippus, in Rubens's painting of their *Abduction*. But it is not merely a question of the borrowing of a single form. It is for the richly sensual approach to flesh and materials, whose life-enhancing lavishness is so alien to destruction, that Rubens's work was the fundamental – indeed, the most potent possible – source. (Joannides, in ibid.: 150)

It is also arguable that, while the oriental focus in both films may have predominantly sexual motivations, Robbe-Grillet's representation of it has a self-consciously de-realising effect which empties it of ideological significance, and that as we have seen, the Orient has an uncanny status, generating sensations of familiarity and strangeness that, together with other features of the *mise-en-scène*, invite us to put in question the very nature of the real.

At the level of the creative act, however, the consequence of the lessening of restraints on Robbe-Grillet in relation to the depiction of the sexual and the increasing inclusion in his films of soft-core and mild yet overt sadomasochistic imagery has been an impoverishment of the aesthetic, as a personal sexual impetus has been given freer rein. What may work well in the finely honed descriptive passages of his novels appears simply crude on the cinema screen.[29] *L'Immortelle*, in which the fetishistic and the sadomasochistic have a more muted presence, is superior to *Gradiva* in this respect, the horrors of explicit representation subordinated to a more complex psychosexual exploration. Paradoxically, the constraints of censorship in the early 1960s led to a greater subtlety that was ultimately more artistically successful.

References

Athanassoglou-Kallmyer, Nina (2001), 'Eugène Delacroix and Popular Culture', in Beth S. Wright (ed.), *The Cambridge Companion to Delacroix*, 48–68.

Berger, John (1985 [1972]), *Ways of Seeing*, London, British Broadcasting Corporation and Penguin Books.

Burch, Noël (2005), 'Retour sur *L'Immortelle*', in Prédal, *Robbe-Grillet Cinéaste*, 25–33.

Fragola, Anthony N. and Smith, Roch C. (1992), *The Erotic Dream Machine: Interviews with Alain Robbe-Grillet on His Films*, Carbondale and Edwardsville, Southern Illinois University Press.

Freud, Sigmund (1984a [1972]), 'Fetishism', in Pelican Freud Library 7: *On Sexuality*, Harmondsworth, Penguin Books, 345–57.

Freud, Sigmund (1984b [1920]), *Beyond the Pleasure Principle*, Harmondsworth, Penguin, Pelican Freud Library, vol. 11.

Freud, Sigmund (1985a [1919]), 'Das Unheimliche'; trans.'The Uncanny', in *Art and Literature*, Harmondsworth, Middlesex, Pelican Freud Library 14, Penguin Books, 335–76.

Freud, Sigmund (1985b [1907]), 'Delusions and Dreams in Jensen's *Gradiva*', in *Art and Literature*, Harmondsworth, Middlesex, Pelican Freud Library 14, Penguin Books, 27–118.

Gallet, Pascal-Emmanuelle (ed.) (1982), *Alain Robbe-Grillet: Œuvres Cinématographiques*, Édition vidéographique critique, Paris, Ministère des relations extérieures, Cellule d'animation culturelle.

Grigsby, Darcy Grimaldo (2001), 'Orients and Colonies: Delacroix's Algerian Harem', in Beth S. Wright (ed.), *The Cambridge Companion to Delacroix*, 69–87.

Joannides, Paul (2001), 'Delacroix and Modern Literature', in Beth S. Wright (ed.), *The Cambridge Companion to Delacroix*, 130–53.

Prédal, René (2005), 'Pompéi, Delacroix et la Maison de rendez-vous du Triangle d'or: *C'est Gradiva qui vous appelle*', in *Robbe-Grillet Cinéaste*,

---

29 The more 'hard-core' representations of other recent French films ironically avoid this effect by being presented from a feminine point of view: see, for example, Catherine Breillat's *Romance* (1999).

Études publiées sous la direction de René Prédal, Caen, Presses universitaires de Caen, 145–55.

Ramsay, Raylene (1992), *Robbe-Grillet and Modernity: Science, Sexuality and Subversion*, Gainesville, University Press of Florida.

Robbe-Grillet, Alain (1963a), 'Temps et description dans le récit d'aujourd'hui', in *Pour un nouveau roman*, Paris, Éditions de Minuit, 123–34.

Robbe-Grillet, Alain (1963b), *L'Immortelle*, Paris, Éditions de Minuit.

Robbe-Grillet, Alain (2002), *C'est Gradiva qui vous appelle*, Paris, Éditions de Minuit.

Robbe-Grillet, Alain (2005), *Préface à une vie d'écrivain*, Paris, France Culture, Éditions du Seuil.

Rubin, James H. (2001), 'Delacroix and Romanticism', in Beth S. Wright (ed.), *The Cambridge Companion to Delacroix*, 26–47.

Saïd, Edward W. (2003 [1978]), *Orientalism*, London, Penguin Books.

Stoltzfus, Ben (1985), *Alain Robbe-Grillet: The Body of the Text*, London and Toronto, Associated University Presses.

ten-Doesschate Chu, Petra (2001), '"A Science and Art at Once": Delacroix's Pictorial Theory and Practice', in Beth S. Wright (ed.), *The Cambridge Companion to Delacroix*, 88–107.

Wolfreys, Julian (2007), *Derrida: A Guide for the Perplexed*, London and New York, Continuum Books.

Wright, Beth S. (ed.), (2001) *The Cambridge Companion to Delacroix*, Cambridge, Cambridge University Press.

Žižek, Slavoj (2002), *Welcome to the Desert of the Real! Five Essays on September 11 and Related Dates*, London, Verso.

Zootrope Films (2006), *Les Films du Lendemain and Z Company Publicity Pamphlet*.

5

Sado-eroticism:
Trans-Europ-Express, *L'Eden et après*, *Glissements progressifs du plaisir*

Je n'ai jamais parlé d'autre chose que de moi.[1] (Robbe-Grillet, *Le Miroir qui revient*)

Up until the 1980s, critics generally espoused the view, encouraged by the author himself, that the world created in Robbe-Grillet's work bore little or no resemblance to the real world, and the text was to be regarded as non-mimetic and non-referential, as art not life. Like the novels, the films did not offer us real locations to be identified from our personal experience, nor were the sexual elements to be confused with reality, Robbe-Grillet's universe being an essentially imaginary creation, a mix of stereotype and personal fantasy.[2] Since the 1980s, when the writer himself became far less guarded about his sexuality and its influence on his work, it has become difficult to maintain such a view.[3] However, both the nature and function of sexual imagery in his films and continuing critical responses to them are complex and demand careful consideration both in this and the final chapter.

Robbe-Grillet's sexual obsessions led him to draw heavily in his cinematic œuvre on popular cultural sources, particularly on 'soft-core' films of the 1960s and 1970s, and this strategy has at times led

---

1 'All I've ever talked about is myself'
2 Generally speaking, with the notable exception of Raylene Ramsay, this has been the view of critics sympathetic to the author/director. Ben Stoltzfus, for example: 'for the reader to be offended or titillated signifies an egregious misreading of a text in which women's bodies, as in *La Belle Captive*, are no more than metaphors for language and, therefore, as unreal as the mannikins [*sic*] that Robbe-Grillet frequently substitutes for them' (1985: 76).
3 See the beginning of Chapter 6 for a fuller discussion of Robbe-Grillet's sexual confessions.

feminist critics to tar him with the same brush as the authors of such films. This was the case of all of his films since the 1970s, especially, *Glissements progressifs du plaisir*, and yet, ironically, cinema-goers have on occasions reacted with incomprehension and even anger when their expectations of conventional pornographic images and scenarios in these films were disappointed.[4] Nevertheless, it is undeniable that like the novels, these films contain strong erotic elements. The question of whether their contents may fairly be described as pornographic needs now to be more closely addressed. A related issue concerns the distinction between soft- and hard-core pornography. Both have some bearing on the degree to which his films might be thought to degrade women.

Pornography is conventionally distinguished from erotica as a form of low or popular as opposed to high culture. Robbe-Grillet himself always spoke of eroticism and not pornography, a choice of language designed to position his work ultimately in high culture, satirical intentions justifying the presence of explicit sex and nudity. Robbe-Grillet himself undermines this opposition, however, when he observes that 'La pornographie, c'est l'érotisme des autres'[5] (Pauvert 1994: 59). These terms are, in other words, wholly subjective and frequently politically motivated.[6]

Such distinctions, based as they are on historical and cultural variables, are therefore highly unstable. The most one can do is identify historical trends. Thus, for Tanya Krzywinska, the sex films of the 1970s, designed for mainstream consumption, were essentially soft-core:

> The gauzy soft-focus visual style of *Bilitis* (1977) [...] Even the bondage and domination film *Story of O* (*Histoire d'O*, 1975), which focuses on the initiation of a woman into the intense pleasures of sexual submission, is mostly shot in soft focus [...] This approach lends the film's more violent scenes visual sensuality rather than brutal realism. It also ties into the film's attempt to capture the imaginary nature of sexual

4 When the 1974 film, *Glissements progressifs du plaisir* was released in Italy, there were public disturbances bordering on riots in some cinemas among audiences who had been led by the title and by poster images to expect conventional soft porn.

5 'Pornography is what other people find erotic'

6 See Phillips 1999: 4–7, for a more in-depth discussion of the erotica–pornography debate.

fantasy, where what would, in reality, be deeply unpleasant becomes in the world of make-believe the source of sensual pleasure. In keeping with its soft-core aesthetic, *The Story of O* deals with the erotics of submission in a highly idealised way in aesthetic and narrative terms. (2006: 33)

Krzywinska argues that hard distinguishes itself from soft core 'mainly through its promise to portray authentic rather than simulated sex' (ibid.: 47–8). Hard core, however, has also been aimed at a popular if much more limited market.

If we are to give Robbe-Grillet's eroticism a label on the basis of Krzywinska's definitions, then, the sexual images of his films are soft not hard: plenty of breasts, buttocks and pubic hair are readily visible, but soft focus is frequently employed and both female and male genitals remain hidden from view, and while naked women are tied to bed posts, there are no shots of penetration. This does not in itself make the films mainstream – indeed, a mass audience would find the absence of a linear realist plot extremely irritating. But given their resemblance in these respects to typical soft-core films of the 1970s, such as *Emmanuelle*, in which female nudity, sexual acts such as masturbation, lesbianism and sadomasochism were allowed for the first time, Robbe-Grillet's soft-core eroticism does superficially have a popular flavour, and indeed, looks hackneyed in 2010. Even the erotic elements of his last film, *C'est Gradiva qui vous appelle*, do not in themselves manifest innovatory qualities. There is, for example, no evidence of any influence of recent trends towards the exploratory use of hard core from an artistic point of view, as seen in other French films of the last two decades which contain shots of erect penises and close-ups on vaginas.[7] Given these trends in art-house French cinema, *Gradiva* could have gone much further down the road of explicitness in an artistic context. His work has not fundamentally changed in this respect over the years. *Glissements* and *La Belle captive*, films of the 1970s and 1980s, were in this sense more of their time.

---

7 *Romance* (1999) and *Baise-moi* (2000) are probably the most memorable examples of this trend.

Erotic influences

In harmony with the *Emmanuelle* trend of mainstream soft-core cinema in the 1970s, Robbe-Grillet's eroticism also seems influenced by both Gothic and Hitchcockian melodrama. We may distinguish between Gothic melodrama and horror on the one hand and Hitchcock-type film noir on the other, the latter having acquired a 'highbrow' status in film criticism, whereas the former are popular cultural genres. Robbe-Grillet's borrowings display elements of both.

The vampiric scenes in *La Belle captive*, and the secret chambers in *Gradiva* in which beautiful young women are raped and tortured and possibly murdered echo eighteenth- and nineteenth-century Gothic novels, in particular those of the Marquis de Sade, and popular twentieth-century horror films. They also have traces of a tongue-in-cheek humour, that makes one think of recent television shows such as *Buffy the Vampire Slayer* and *Supernatural*. All such features and motifs are vulnerable to parody, or respectful imitation of an artistic nature which could have lifted them into a higher cultural category, but there is no real evidence of this in the narrative of these films.

On the other hand, the construction of the detective story plots in *La Belle captive* and other films relies heavily on classic Hitchcockian devices: the scrambling of dream and reality, the creation of enigmas to be resolved in an atmosphere of increasing mystery and tension, the laying of false trails, the role of unconscious desires, and the circularity of the filmic structure all suggest an affectionate parody of the genre. René Prédal compares *Gradiva*, for example, with *Vertigo* (2005: 148), and I argued in Chapter 4 that the basic plot structure of *L'Immortelle* also recalls this film. Moreover, Hitchcock's penchant for blonde actresses is found in the focus in both narratives on a mysterious blonde who appears and disappears, and may or may not be the mortal victim of a male sex crime. In response to an enquiry by the hero of *Gradiva*, John, as to the numbers of young blonde women in this part of the world, Anatoli emphasises their rarity and consequent value as erotic objects:

> Il ne devait pas y avoir beaucoup de jeunes femmes blondes dans ces contrées! – Parmi les natives, non, et c'est ce qui en faisait le prix. On en vendait malgré tout fréquemment, très cher, sur les marchés aux esclaves. Vous connaissez la scène, qui figure dans de nombreux tableaux orientalistes! Le goût pour la chair blanche était fort répandu et tous les riches harems comportaient quelques odalisques aux yeux

pâles qui en étaient le fleuron. Les jolies rousses venaient de Circassie ou d'Irlande. Des pirates enlevaient des adolescentes blondes jusque sur les côtes de Norvège.[8] (Robbe-Grillet 2002: 46–7)

Even Robbe-Grillet's use of the film noir, however, is complex: not crudely parodic nor simply a homage to its best exponents, even Hitchcock. One might best describe it as an artistic borrowing, but sex is never very far away. In the past, the erotic contents of Robbe-Grillet's novels have been partly justified, as I have suggested, on satirical grounds but, as Roch C. Smith implies in his questioning of the author, sado-erotic scenes may be designed above all to exorcise the monsters that haunt him (Fragola and Smith 1992: 144). Even this personal eroticism is argued to assume an aesthetic dimension. In a preface to the English translation of the 1970 novel, *Projet pour une révolution à New York*, the author declares:

> I establish a relationship between three types of crime: political, or regicide; sexual, or the rape and murder of a young woman; and textual, or the New Novel. I establish a parallel between the social body, the woman's body, and the body of the narrative [...] erotic material serves as a nod to one of the originators of cinema, who, when asked what the cinema was, responded that it consists of doing pretty things to pretty women. (Robbe-Grillet 1973: Preface)

This is a clever, nay humorous attempt to mask the sexual with the textual, but the mask is paper thin. Like the humour, Robbe-Grillet's consistently high public profile may be thought an important part of a defensive authorial strategy of response to negative criticism. It is, after all, unusual for an author to talk as much about himself in conferences, interviews and theoretical publications as Robbe-Grillet does.

How may we reconcile this personal dimension with Robbe-Grillet's repeated insistence on the formalistic? Roland Barthes speculated that all writers play with their mother's body (1973: 60). This notion

---

8 '"There can't have been many young blonde women in these parts!" "No, not among the natives, and that's what made them valuable. They were often sold for quite high prices at the slave markets. You know the scene. You can find it in numerous orientalist paintings! The taste for white flesh was quite widespread and all of the rich harems prided themselves on including a few pale-eyed odalisques. The pretty redheads came from Circassia or Ireland. Pirates kidnapped adolescent blonde women from places as far north as the coasts of Norway."'

directly links the ludic, the personal and the erotic, and so potentially, the formalistic and the sexual. The writer may be both lewd
and innovative at the same time. In Robbe-Grillet's case, this 'lewdo'-
eroticism takes a fetishistic and a masochistic form. Like Sade, he
claims to identify above all with his female characters who tend to be
victimised either by societal institutions such as the law or the church,
or by individual male figures. While he accepts that he has 'sadistic'
impulses, sadomasochism, however, he suggests, 'merely constitutes
the material to be used [in his work] In our societies, sadomasochism
is an erotic stereotype [...] Sade proposes sadomasochism in the name
of nature against the word of society, whereas I take up the sadomasochistic images within the latent discourse of society, the astonishing
cultural stereotypes of society' (Fragola and Smith 1992: 82).[9]

Stereotypes

Ostensibly, Robbe-Grillet is recycling society's sexual stereotypes (in
the same way that he does racial and cultural stereotypes) in parodic
mode. Stoltzfus claims that in this way, Robbe-Grillet plays with the
'forbidden lusts of our society': 'It is censored faces that Robbe-Grillet
displays in his novels and films, staging oneiric dramas in that space
where the conflict between illicit desire and the symbols of the establishment come together' (1985: 144). He attacks stereotype, critics have
argued, because it is the facile reliance on stereotype that is closely
linked to the dangers of repression and that he sees as all-pervasive
in our culture. His use of these stereotypes is equivalent, therefore,
to transforming the signifieds of erotic arousal into the signifiers
of a parody of such processes: 'La société dans laquelle nous vivons
est de toute évidence construite sur des mythes [...] Ce que j'utilise
comme matériau c'est justement ce matériel thématique des mythes
contemporains, et, par conséquent, l'érotisme puisqu'il en est une
des composantes les plus remarquables'[10] (Robbe-Grillet 2005: 129).

9 The stereotypical character of these images has already been discussed in the
   context of the films' oriental settings in Chapter 4. Their discussion here will
   focus on the erotic. As I argued in the last chapter, there is an element of disin-
   genuousness in his claims to be using such imagery for purely artistic purposes.
10 'The society in which we live is clearly built on myths [...] The material I use is
   precisely this thematic material from contemporary myths, and consequently,
   eroticism since this is one of its most remarkable components.'

The myths and stereotypes of our culture, then, provide the raw material, as it were, for the sculpting of a model of the real. Stoltzfus explains how the title of Robbe-Grillet's third film itself signposts the parody of detective-story and erotic stereotypes: 'In *Trans-Europ-Express*, for instance, a title that connotes *Fear, Sex*, and *Death*, the word *Trans* slips into *transes* (meaning "fears"). *Europ*, the Paris to Antwerp train, becomes *Europe*, a girlie magazine. *Express* is simultaneously the train and the name of a news magazine, featuring "L'Homme qui est mort quatre fois" (The Man Who Died Four Times)' (1985: 76).

Admittedly, there is frequently a framing of the erotic imagery which has a distancing effect. This framing is partly intertextual, in that we are confronted here with stereotypes that punctuate the entire Robbe-Grillet corpus (pretty young girls, blonde hair, half-open mouths, blue eyes). These stereotypes are always employed with self-conscious irony.

In *Trans-Europ-Express*, for example, the actor Trintignant, alias Mathias (the name of the paedophile and murder suspect of *Le Voyeur*), alias Jean, follows the beautiful spy and prostitute, Eva, to her room, ties her wrists to the bed, 'rapes' her – she appears to enjoy this – to music from Verdi's *La Traviata* (which is itself the story of a prostitute), then strangles her. Both characters are inspired by a bondage magazine, hidden between the covers of *L'Express*, that Trintignant is reading on the Trans-Europ-*Express* (my emphasis).

Similarly, *L'Eden*, Robbe-Grillet argues, attacks the very stereotypes that imprison women in roles (and myths) constructed by men:

> A young woman is caught up in a society that is visibly macho. As you know, those societies exist. They are not my invention. This young woman will then be tormented by macho myths: triumphant virility, woman as object, and so forth. At the beginning of the film she seems to respect this ideology, and the first time she comes upon the mass of sperm oozing from machinery in the factory, she touches it with fear and respect. The entire evolution of the film will be the story of her liberation, for at the end she gathers up the sperm again – which is nothing more than white glue – covers herself with it and laughs. She also violently slaps this man who represents macho qualities. The only real violence in the film is that slap. What could be better? [...] The students play at rape, but obviously, that rape is not realistic and certainly no more realistic than the scene of poisoning and burial that occurs later [...] it would be an error to see the film as realistic. (Fragola and Smith 1992: 60–1)

This has also been the view shared by critics closest to the author, but it is too often undermined by the very potential to arouse that such imagery possesses. Though the heroine of *L'Eden* appears to insist on her autonomy, she is unavoidably objectified, not only by the male and sometimes female characters of the film, but also, and most significantly, as the focus of the camera lens: miniskirted, with knee-length leather boots, object of male play-rape, a ravishingly beautiful young woman stripped naked in numerous scenes, she can hardly escape the male spectator's gaze. Shots of her shirt made diaphanous by the seawater, making her ample breasts and dark nipples and areolae starkly visible, provide the most striking example of her role as sexual object.

Robbe-Grillet is clearly and by his own admission himself implicated in these stereotypes of the erotic. I shall pursue this argument with particular reference to the film that has raised it more obviously than any other: *Glissements progressifs du plaisir*.

Glissements progressifs du plaisir

Riding the crest of a new wave of liberalism in the cinema, *Glissements* is probably Robbe-Grillet's most daring exercise in screen nudity and eroticism. At all significant levels, the film turns upon the feminine as the source of eroticism, and as such, follows a long and complex tradition in French cinema and above all, French literature traceable back to the seventeenth century, a tradition of which the film contains recognisable echoes (see n. 11). This is also the most transparently parodic of his films, satirising both cinematic realism and sexual hypocrisy in society's most respected institutions.

Robbe-Grillet originally named the heroine of the film Anicée since the film had been written for her, but the actress did not want to be identified, so he used the name Alice instead. Fortuitously, she does recall *Alice in Wonderland*: in both narratives, Alice is a young innocent who exposes the characters she encounters as ridiculous and/or self-serving.

As in all of the films, the plot is at once simple and complex. A girl has been found at home by the police in the presence of the corpse of a young woman. Alice is accused of having murdered the woman and is locked up in a correction house for minors, run by nuns and priests. She is interrogated by a judge who has collected all the clues picked up by a policeman, a bumbling, Inspector Clouzot-type figure. The material evidence consists of objects found in the apartment: a pair of blue shoes, a broken bottle, a kneeler and other objects that do not seem associated with a criminal act. As in conventional French police dramas, the judge is charged with constructing the story of the crime out of this disparate set of objects. His role is therefore to make a narrative out of them in the realist sense, such that the girl can be found guilty of the crime. Robbe-Grillet is reacting here against Balzacian constructions of meaning in the clues assembled. Alice rejects this version of reality in the same way that the author refuses a realism that he views as a con trick, and so refuses to cooperate with the investigation process. The whole film is on the narrative level the story of the interrogation and reconstitution of the crime, but at every turn, Alice undermines the construction of meaning. Her accusers succumb to her naked charms, and in this sense, she constitutes an inversion of the realist male murder suspect.

In similar vein, Robbe-Grillet's prison is symbolic rather than realist. Alice is held in a white room with little furniture and bare walls, not unlike certain contemporary styles of interior decoration, a pure, white cell, staffed by nuns in virginal white robes. This unconventional prison contrasts sharply with the dark vaults below, in which the sexual fantasies of the male authority figures in the film (policeman, magistrate, priest) are acted out, implying that these are the real prisoners. This spatial verticality symbolises the sexual repression in the unconscious of the celibate clergy.[11]

Both spaces are kinds of prison, however, since both, whether actually or metaphorically, function to repress: 'La prison est un fantasme récurrent dans ces films [...] et c'est probablement un fantasme masculin assez répandu [...] C'est lui-même qui est prison-

11 The prison in which Alice is held recalls the main location of the 1683 erotic novel, *Vénus dans le cloître ou, La religieuse en chemise* by abbé Du Prat. There are also echoes of Sade's *Justine, ou les malheurs de la vertu*, in which the eponymous heroine is incarcerated by the lascivious monks of Sainte Marie des Bois, and of the main representatives of male order (justice, nobility, church, high finance) of his *Les 120 Journées de Sodome* – in Robbe-Grillet's film, justice, church, police. In ironic homage to the Marquis de Sade, much of the film was shot in the Château de Vincennes, one of the many prisons in which Sade was himself locked up, and in fact, in the same cell where Sade was kept (Fragola and Smith 1992: 81).

nier de ses fantasmes ʼ[12] (Gallet 1982: 55). The priest is obsessed by lesbianism and the torture of young girls – shades of the Inquisition – and the young 'witch' feeds his fantasies, which Robbe-Grillet admits are his own.

The film's narrative structure is therefore based on the principle of slippage, Robbe-Grillet's aim being:

> to make a film in which the narration is intercut with punctuation shots that serve to separate the scenes. Little by little, slippages occur from the punctuation shots towards the narration, from the narration towards the punctuation shots, and from one scene to another through the intermediary of punctuation. Punctuation shots, whose origins are 'tailpieces' in typography and 'fades' in film, are gradually integrated into the narration. There is a structural slippage from punctuation shots towards the diegesis. The structural idea was, in short, this concept of slippage. (Fragola and Smith 1992: 70)

There is thus not so much a single narrative thread as a series of what Anthony Fragola calls 'narrative possibilities' (ibid.: 71). Robbe-Grillet again:

> The judge always wants to simplify matters, to tell a coherent story, but the pieces of evidence are not coherent; some people lie or do not remember, while others contradict previous testimony [...] [*Glissements*] is simply a question of an extreme case where the accused person undermines the telling of the story, the roles, and, of course, meaning in general. (Ibid.)

In this sense, the judge represents the traditional storyteller that Robbe-Grillet rejects.

As the film title suggests, it is thus the slippage of meanings that Alice both linguistically and symbolically represents that is the main instrument of subversion in *Glissements*. The topos of slippage is directly worked out here, informing the narrative at literal and above all, metaphorical levels. The 'slippages' of the title refer above all to the ways in which Alice uses words perversely, inventing a succession of crazy stories, and taking language into a Wonderland worthy of Lewis Carroll. Judge, priest and policeman can find no secure footholds in a fantastic world created by a nonsense language, both verbal and visual, in which realism and order have no purchase.

12 'The prison is a recurrent fantasy in these films [...] and is probably a common male fantasy [...] it is he himself who is a prisoner of those fantasies'

These slippages of language are reflected in slippages between objects (eggs, a broken bottle, the shoe, a piece of rope, the scissors, the foot or hand of the mannequin, the shovel, the unbroken bottle containing the folded message), from one object to another, and from objects to the narrative and back. Slippage is what the judge fears most. He would like to create meaning from all these objects which constantly threaten the order he so desperately seeks to protect.[13] These slippages of signifiers and their signifieds are metaphorically echoed in other, less concrete forms of slippage: spatially, for example, in the role of the sea, and the shot of a girl slipping off the cliff; temporally, as linear time is undermined by the circularity of references to the objects mentioned above. Slippage does, of course, also have sexual connotations, especially when juxtaposed, as it is in the film title, with the word *plaisir* ('pleasure'). Slippage finally is seen to lead to catharsis in an incantatory and metonymic sequence at the end of the film, in which Alice pronounces the key words of a narrative of liberation which is also a celebration of slippage and its subversive power ('Jeu. Viol. Plaisir. Structure. Infraction. Sperme. Dédouble-ment. Permutation'[14] (Robbe-Grillet 1974: 140). The girl-witch is seen standing, looking out at the sea: 'Ce plan devrait être tourné dans une lumière rose de crépuscule et durer assez longtemps. Bruits joyeux de vent, de mer et de mouettes: la liberté'[15] (ibid.: 141). This apparently euphoric dénouement is described here in the very terms of cliché and stereotype that are rejected on other levels – an implication, perhaps, that slippage is everywhere.

There may even be slippage at the level of (authorial) intentionality, Robbe-Grillet's oft-stated view being that since men have rape fantasies, it is better to talk about them. In *Glissements*, religious repression is not merely hinted at but literalised, as nuns perform cunnilingus on each other in the 'dark prison', and Alice invites the priest to bite and scratch her, exorcise her, crush her breasts with his hands, as the priest writhes in a mixture of agony and ecstasy. All of these scenes, it is implied, may be taking place in the repressed fantasies of their protagonists, as may a highly erotic scene in which eggs are cracked over Nora's naked body, an intertextual echo of

13 The links between objects and disorder are further explored in Chapter 6.
14 'Game. Rape. Pleasure. Structure. Infraction. Sperm. Doubling. Permutation'
15 'This shot should be done in the pink light of dusk and last quite a long time. Joyous sounds of the wind, the sea and the seagulls: freedom.'

Georges Bataille's *Histoire de l'œil* (*Story of the Eye*, 1928). Bataille's novel similarly appears to attack the repression of sexual impulses while also inevitably appealing to the reader's prurient interest in their representation.

Glissements was inspired by Roland Barthes's reading of Michelet's *La Sorcière* in his *Michelet par lui-même* (see Barthes 1965 and Robbe-Grillet 1987: 206ff.). Michelet attributes sexual repression to the white male, whereas he sees the young woman as the spirit of freedom and symbol of the French Revolution. Thus, Alice rebels against the chief representatives of order in French society – judge, priest and policeman. For the author, her naked body represents a non-conformism that threatens the established order. As Stoltzfus argues, '*Glissements progressifs du plaisir* is nothing less than a triumph of the id, a victory of the pleasure principle over the representatives of law and order, the repressive types of establishment superego' (1985: 144).

Although Michelet was on the side of the young witch, he was also obsessed by the blood of women, and, Robbe-Grillet maintains, takes an obvious pleasure in the torture of the beautiful young woman, and indeed, the images of burning in the film clearly recall the burning of witches. Moreover, Robbe-Grillet's 'witch' is subjected to a number of symbolic interrogations and 'tortures' that are intensely eroticised. The police inspector, the priest, the judge and even her lawyer who is a woman are seen to possess, and perhaps to act on sadistic impulses towards the ever-naked Alice. There are frequent images of cutting and bloodsucking, which appear to repeat the acts of violence for which she herself has been imprisoned. Metaphorically put to the question, Alice heroically resists sexual objectification, however, turning the table on her inquisitors who are themselves made to suffer from the consequences of their sexual repression. For Robbe-Grillet, 'she upsets the masculine order not only with her body but also through her reasoning by which she undercuts the logic of a police investigation' (Fragola and Smith 1992: 70). She destroys the three representatives of order by rejecting that which alone can save them: order itself. For example, the judge tries to cling to the code of laws. In one scene, inspired by Orson Welles's adaptation of Kafka's *The Trial*, the judge is in bed surrounded by law books, uttering single abstractions in a stream of non sequiturs, as if on the verge of a mental breakdown. The girl-witch has finally destroyed the meaning of the words in his dictionaries, and in the process, has destroyed both him and the repressive laws he represents (Gallet 1982: 52). The priest who takes a visible sexual pleasure in torturing the young girl is seen to be destroyed by his own fantasies. Michelet tells us that in the Middle Ages the unmarried woman was an object of scandal, since she was considered to be in league with the devil if she was young and beautiful. Such a woman was perceived as a threat to social and moral stability. In *Glissements*, it is indeed the heroine who represents the focus of opposition to male repression, and is seen to triumph over the men.

Nevertheless, feminist critics attacked the film for its objectification of the female body, and it was even censored in Italy for reasons which Robbe-Grillet ridiculed with characteristic irony:

> The judge was right from the point of view of a judge (as defender of order), and the sorceress was right from the point of view of freedom [...] My lawyer said that the judge did not have a right to pronounce a judgement on this affair since it was, in fact, his own fantasies that he had put into the film. One of the articles of the law maintains that one cannot be at the same time a judge and an interested party. Well, he is an interested party, and so, in fact, he cannot judge. The court was beside itself. (Fragola and Smith 1992: 73)

The grounds upon which the Italian judge banned the film was, Robbe-Grillet argued, 'non-narrativity'. He found this judgment ironic on three counts: first, that a film which celebrates the spirit of feminine revolution should be accused of being a macho, anti-feminist work; second, that the film should have been condemned for 'outraging morals' in Italy (the judges condemned Robbe-Grillet for the same reasons that the witch is condemned, and like the witch, the film was ordered to be burned); and third, the judge understood nothing about the plot, and so could find nothing to justify the erotic scenes which could have been tolerated only if considered essential to it, and therefore, the film was found to be pornographic (Gallet 1982: 52–3). In Bologna, where the film was banned, spectators rioted and destroyed the cinema when their expectations of sadistic porn, encouraged by the lurid Italian posters for the film, were disappointed. For Robbe-Grillet, they were so shocked by the narrative that they condemned the film for non-narrativity, just like the Italian judge: 'Lovers of pornography', he claimed, 'are on the side of repressive justice' (ibid: 55). The author's ostensibly parodic intentions notwithstanding, *Glissements* goes much further than any other film in the corpus in its inclusion of voyeurism of an explicitly sexual nature. Alice, the young and nubile murder suspect, spends most of her time naked.[16] It is hardly surprising therefore that a succession of men, and some nuns with lesbian tendencies, are drawn to spy on her. Voyeuristic pleasure is undeniably on the menu, then, but may be vindicated by appealing to both sexes.

For Laura Mulvey (1975), only the male spectator experiences pleasure, through visual enjoyment of the female star, as he shares the voyeuristic gaze of the camera and the male star, with whom he identifies. Through this process, the male spectator is able to neutralise the castration anxiety that the female image always evokes: his sadistic voyeurism demystifies the female body, while his fetishistic scopophilia turns it into a substitute for the missing phallus. The female spectator, on the other hand, has nothing to look at and no one to identify with. Since Mulvey's seminal essay, feminist film critics have repeatedly problematised the pleasure of the female spectator. 'Cinema', declares Mary Ann Doane, for example, 'is about woman, not for her. She is assigned a special place in cinematic representation but denied access to that system' (1992: 760). This is true also of the dominant critical discourse in film studies, psychoanalysis, which places the phallus at the centre of interpretation. So perhaps we need to ask how this film promotes the interests of the female spectator.

The main protagonist in *Glissements*, Alice, is a woman, and even when she is not the agent of sexual activity, other women are – Nora/ Alice's lawyer, Sister Julia and other nuns in the convent. Regardless of gender or sexuality, then, it is not inconceivable that the spectator may move between different positions, identifying with one character's sadism or with another's masochism (men and women occupy both positions), shifting from active to passive as much as from male to female positions. Masochistic and even sadistic fantasy might also be thought of as liberating for women in that, as Linda Williams suggests, 'it may represent for women a new consciousness about the unavoidable role of power in sex, gender, and sexual representations and of the importance of not viewing this power as fixed' (1990: 228).

16 Despite the fact that Alice Alvina was a minor and not a professional, Robbe-Grillet had an excellent rapport with her, and she was willing to do anything demanded of her, and enjoyed herself, at least, according to him: 'I got along so well with Anicée because she had fun' (Fragola and Smith 1992: 76).

On the other hand, spectators in search of pornographic realism would almost certainly be dismayed to discover that the apparent sado-erotic treatment of young women existed only in their own fantasies. In one short scene, the magistrate peers through a peephole into a room from which he has heard cries of sexual ecstasy or pain. This is a trap both for the 'peeping-tom' magistrate and the spectator, since the sounds are actually coming from a record player on Alice's bed. The scene demonstrates the magistrate's hypocritical and repressed sexuality, the girl's superiority over men in general, and the tenuous character of the real. Like the magistrate, the virtual spectator of pornography is frequently duped into taking representation for reality.

This mischievous scene can be read as a *mise en abyme* of the film as a whole, in which erotic representations slide ambiguously and deceptively between a number of different positions: from a potentially pornographic account of authorial fantasy to a subversive parody of pornographic stereotype to a ludic self-irony which invites the spectator to assist the author-director in deconstructing his own writing project. The author is clearly implicated in the eroticism of these representations, but it would be inaccurate to describe them as pornographic per se. The narrative's numerous thematic and structural slippages undermine the pornographic effect, and indeed, by virtue of a number of distancing devices, help to make the film accessible to the feminist, as well as to the female spectator.

These slippages may also be seen, in a psychoanalytic perspective, as displacement activity, themselves acting as signifiers, standing in for (or more accurately, deflecting attention away from) slippages of a sexual nature. Thus, form and content in fact become inseparable. Irony, parody and satire distance the spectator, but also the writing subject from an anxiety associated with an inability to grasp and keep hold of the object of desire. This anxiety is also the source of powerful controlling tendencies, a feature of the films which will be discussed in detail in the final chapter.

References

Barthes, Roland (1965), *Michelet par lui-même*. Images et textes présentés par Roland Barthes, Écrivains de toujours 19, Éditions du Seuil.
Barthes, Roland (1973), *Le Plaisir du texte*, Paris, Éditions du Seuil, Points.
Bataille, Georges (1970; first publ. 1928), *Histoire de l'œil*, in *Œuvres Complètes*,

vol. 1, Paris, Gallimard.

Doane, Mary Anne (1992 [1982]), 'Film and the Masquerade: Theorising the Female Spectator', in Gerald Mast, Marshall Cohen and Leo Braudy (eds), *Film Theory and Criticism: Introductory Readings*, Oxford, Oxford University Press, 758–72.

Doubrovsky, Serge (1966), *Pourquoi la nouvelle critique?*, Paris, Mercure de France.

Fragola, Anthony N. and Smith, Roch C. (1992), *The Erotic Dream Machine: Interviews with Alain Robbe-Grillet on His Films*, Carbondale and Edwardsville, Southern Illinois University Press.

Gallet, Pascal-Emmanuelle (ed.) (1982), *Alain Robbe-Grillet: Œuvres Cinématographiques*, Édition vidéographique critique, Paris, Ministère des relations extérieures, Cellule d'animation culturelle.

Gardies, André (2005), 'Le travail du double', in Prédal, *Robbe-Grillet Cinéaste*, 105–43.

Krzywinska, Tanya (2006), *Sex and the Cinema*, London and New York, Wallflower Press.

Mulvey, Laura (1975), 'Visual Pleasure and Narrative Cinema', *Screen* 16(3): 6–18.

Pauvert, Jean-Jacques (1994), *Nouveaux visages de la censure*, Paris, Les Belles Lettres.

Phillips, John (1999), *Forbidden Fictions: Pornography and Censorship in Twentieth-century French Literature*, London and Sterling, Virginia, Pluto Press.

Prédal, René (2005), 'Pompéi, Delacroix et la Maison de rendez-vous du Triangle d'or: *C'est Gradiva qui vous appelle*', in *Robbe-Grillet Cinéaste*, Études publiées sous la direction de René Prédal, Caen, Presses universitaires de Caen, 145–55.

Ricardou, Jean (1971), 'La fiction flamboyante', in *Pour une théorie du nouveau roman*, Paris, Éditions du Seuil.

Robbe-Grillet, Alain (1973), Preface, *Project for a Revolution in New York*, London, Calder and Boyars Ltd.

Robbe-Grillet, Alain (1974), *Glissements progressifs du plaisir*, Paris, Éditions de Minuit.

Robbe-Grillet, Alain (1984), *Le Miroir qui revient*, Paris, Éditions de Minuit.

Robbe-Grillet, Alain (1987), *Angélique, ou l'enchantement*, Paris, Éditions de Minuit.

Robbe-Grillet, Alain (2002), *C'est Gradiva qui vous appelle*, Paris, Éditions de Minuit.

Robbe-Grillet, Alain (2005), *Préface à une vie d'écrivain*, Paris, Éditions du Seuil.

Stoltzfus, Ben (1985), *Alain Robbe-Grillet: The Body of the Text*, London and Toronto, Associated University Presses.

Williams, Linda (1990), *Hard Core. Power, Pleasure and the Frenzy of the Visible*, London, Pandora Press.

6

Fetishism and Control:
La Belle captive

As a modernist, Robbe-Grillet had paid lip-service to the notion that any work of art is a collaborative process, and that as Roland Barthes had argued in his influential essay, 'The Death of the Author' (1984), the reader/spectator's contribution to the creative act necessarily reduces that of the author:

> Je ne crois pas que la différence entre l'auteur et le spectateur soit ce qu'elle aurait pu être au XIX siècle. J'ai l'impression que l'œuvre de Balzac se présente comme finie et que le lecteur reste en face; en somme le roman balzacien peut se passer complètement de son lecteur; il n'y a pas de place pour lui dans l'écriture. L'œuvre que je vous propose est au contraire un appel à votre participation créatrice; chacun de vous doit être celui qui fait le film.[1] (Robbe-Grillet quoted by Gardies in Prédal (2005), 143)

Some years later, however, between the 1980s and the 2000s, Robbe-Grillet expressed quite contrary views in a succession of what he termed 'romanesques' or memoirs which were filled with personal reminiscences and readings of his own work. The last of these, *La Reprise*, describes itself as a novel, but like the previous three memoirs, may also be considered as a fictional autobiography.[2] Taken together, these

---

1 'I do not believe that the difference between the author and the spectator is what it might have been in the nineteenth century. I have the impression that Balzac's work offers itself as complete and that the reader is passive, that the Balzacian novel can in fact do without its reader completely, that there is no place for him or her in the writing. The work which I offer you is on the contrary an appeal to your creative participation. Each one of you must be the one who creates the film.'

2 *Le Miroir qui revient* (1984), *Angélique ou l'enchantement* (1987), *Les Derniers jours de Corinthe* (1994), *La Reprise* (2001).

publications, combined with the content of the numerous interviews he has given over the years, are themselves evidence of a powerful controlling instinct. In these documents, he from time to time explicitly refers to the overriding importance of his own place in the creative process: 'c'est en tout cas pour moi seul que j'écris et que je réalise des films [...] On crée toujours pour soi'[3] (Robbe-Grillet 1984: 184).

Robbe-Grillet was certainly capable of chameleon-like behaviour, a trait which he made no effort to conceal, going so far as to pour scorn on his earlier position as champion of the 'dead author'. In an interview in 1990 for a BBC programme on Barthes, for example, he openly ridiculed the idea that the author was dead as *'totalement risible'* ('totally laughable').[4] Indeed, it seems that Robbe-Grillet's spectator must die for the author to rise from the grave.[5] He argues that he is by no means unusual in this respect, since there is in each and every one of us a tension between the desire for freedom on the one hand and the need for control on the other: 'Ce sont en nous deux forces antagonistes, qui entrent sans cesse en jeu l'une et l'autre, à la fois dans notre conscience et au plus profond de notre inconscient'[6] (Robbe-Grillet 1984: 132). While such admissions are completely at odds with Robbe-Grillet's theoretical position in the 1960s and 1970s, the writer cleverly gives his change of attitude a theoretical underpinning:

> J'ai moi-même beaucoup encouragé ces rassurantes niaiseries. Si je me décide aujourd'hui à les combattre, c'est qu'elles me paraissent avoir fait leur temps: elles ont perdu en quelques années ce qu'elles pouvaient avoir de scandaleux, de corrosif, donc de révolutionnaire, pour se ranger dorénavant parmi les idées reçues, alimentant encore le militantisme gnangnan des journaux de mode, mais avec leur place déjà préparée dans le glorieux caveau de famille des manuels de littérature. L'idéologie, toujours masquée, change facilement de figure.[7] (Ibid.: 11)

3 'in any case I write and make films for myself alone [...] One always creates for oneself'
4 See Barthes 1984 and *TV Degree Zero* 1990.
5 Raylene Ramsay refers to Robbe-Grillet's 'aggressive relation with his spectator, who must be "irritated", "forced" to see and listen, even "killed", according to the writer in *Le Miroir qui revient*' (1992: 166).
6 'They are two opposing forces, constantly at work within us all, both in our conscious existence and in the depths of our unconscious.'
7 'I myself have done much to encourage these reassuring idiocies. If I have now decided to fight against them, it is because I feel they've had their day: within

As early as 1975, at a colloquium on Robbe-Grillet at Cérisy-la Salle, the author coined the term 'ideological double' to denote his role of self-critic, but also of promoter of his own work. The concept brilliantly suggests an objective critical distance, at the same time as it masks his desire to control the reception of his novels and films. Robbe-Grillet himself explains the status and function of his 'ideological double' as a sort of devil's advocate, scattered across the paratexts of his work:

> Mais présenter un objet qui mettrait définitivement en péril l'idéologie, à tel point qu'il ne serait jamais vu par personne parce que, justement, on l'aurait censuré au départ, est peut-être pire que d'occulter un peu le travail de l'œuvre par des clins d'œil à la récupération, disposés soit dans l'œuvre, soit, de préférence, dans les prières d'insérer, dans les présentations à la presse, etc., afin que l'œuvre ne soit pas enterrée et qu'un public plus averti qui la verra autrement puisse se développer.[8] (Ricardou 1976: 162; quoted by Gardies 2005: 105)

Robbe-Grillet's view now, therefore, was that the work should create its own public, a public receptive to its novelty, and for whom the 'ideological double' would, where necessary, serve as guide, by throwing suggestive 'winks' at the spectator from time to time.

This self-exegesis is also a notable trend in public conferences and talks by the author, and in such contexts, is an admirable characteristic. I have often been struck by Robbe-Grillet's clarity and grasp of intellectual concepts, by his rhetorical mastery and his ability to hold an audience for long periods, extemporising without notes, entertaining rapt listeners with tangential anecdotes, and above all, making difficult aspects of his work more comprehensible. A master of self-promotion, Robbe-Grillet understood better than most writers or directors the importance in the modern age of establishing and maintaining a close relationship with his target readers and spectators, more cynically put,

---

the space of a few years they have lost any shocking, corrosive, and therefore revolutionary force they once had, and will henceforth be regarded as clichés, feeding the gutless militancy of the fashionable journals, while their place is already prepared for them in the glorious family vaults of the literary textbooks. When ideology is always masked, it changes face with ease.'

8 'But to present an object that would definitively place an ideology in peril to the point that no one would ever see it because it would have been censured from the start is perhaps worse than to hide some of what is going on in a work by winks scattered either throughout the work itself or, preferably, in inserted notes, press interviews, etc., so that the work is not buried and a more aware public who will see it in a different light can be reached.'

of manipulating the media for his own ends. The screen media, he was quick to realise, were far more powerful than the written word.

Though not given explicit voice until the mid-1970s, this controlling tendency is nevertheless evident as early as 1972 in a brief essay by André Gardies which carried the revealing title, 'Le cinéma selon Robbe-Grillet' (in Gardies, 1972). The text of Gardies's essay was largely rewritten by Robbe-Grillet himself before publication. A comparison between Gardies's original text on the subject, and that modified and corrected by Robbe-Grillet makes the point (changes are indicated in italics):

> Le cinéma a ceci de fascinant, qu'il est en communication directe, en particulier pour les jeunes générations. Il a un pouvoir d'agression érotique très supérieur à celui de la phrase. Il y a une fascination de l'écran qui est effectivement intéressante et dont il faut tenir compte.[9] (Gardies text, 112)

> Le cinéma a ceci de *passionnant*, qu'il e*xerce une action directe sur le public*, en particulier pour les jeunes générations. Il a un pouvoir d'agression très supérieur a celui de la phrase écrite. Il y a une fascination de l'écran, qui est *un phénomène intéressant*, et dont il faut tenir compte.[10] (Version of Gardies text, corrected by Robbe-Grillet, 113)

Robbe-Grillet's remarkable attention to the minutiae of Gardies's account and detailed corrections ironically duplicate the obsessive detail of descriptions in his novels (in the opening pages of *La Jalousie*, for example). They are also evidence of both a strongly didactic streak and a self-defensive strategy. The growing eroticism of his films, in particular, which provoked a negative reception in feminist circles and some censorship, as we saw in the last chapter, seemed to require a defence on artistic grounds.[11]

This tension, then, between, on the one hand, a theoretical liberation of meaning in art, as expressed by Barthes, that it is the reader

---

9 'What is fascinating about the cinema is that it is a form of direct communication, especially for the younger generation. It has an erotic impact that is far superior to that of the sentence. The screen exercises a fascination which is indeed of interest and which must be taken into account.'

10 'What is *absolutely gripping* about the cinema is that it *exercises a direct influence on the public*, especially on the younger generation. It has an impact that is far superior to that of the *written* sentence. The screen exercises a fascination which is *an interesting phenomenon* and which must be taken into account.'

11 Gardies notes the large number of additions and modifications made by Robbe-Grillet to his text whenever this question arose (ibid.: 109).

who creates meaning in interaction with the text, and on the other, a reluctance in practice to deny or downgrade the importance of the author, can be found retrospectively to be at the heart of all Robbe-Grillet's work, and is relevant to the reception of its more controversial aspects. Critics sympathetic to the author have often reiterated his view, for example, that those who have condemned the sexual and in particular, the sadomasochistic contents of the films, have failed to understand their complex structures or their ironic and satirical character. There is clearly some contradiction here between these two positions. In the main, however, Robbe-Grillet's cinematic practice does appear to confirm the dominance of the personal and his need to control, a tendency evident at all of the main stages of film-making, from scripting and shooting to editing.[12]

Shooting

The costly process of shooting is largely shaped by the funds available, but is also a collaborative activity in which the director's artistic control may be challenged by other professionals, by the cinematographer, or by lighting and sound technicians. For these reasons, Robbe-Grillet preferred to limit the shooting process as much as possible. Robbe-Grillet's wary attitude to improvisation by actors, too, is further evidence of his controlling instinct: 'I do not really like the term to improvise, because improvisation seems to imply that the actor has the liberty to say whatever he pleases. On the contrary, I find it important that the actors recite the text exactly as it is written' (Fragola and Smith 1992: 52–3). The actor may occasionally be allowed to intervene creatively, but his intervention is adjusted during the editing process. Robbe-Grillet calls this 'freedom under surveillance' (ibid.: 75). Admittedly, this antipathy to improvisation is also dictated by budgetary concerns: 'What is costly is a cinematographer [...] everyone is paid on the basis of time' (ibid.: 127). Hence, *Marienbad* was completed with exceptional speed, in less than a month, and in the case of *L'Immortelle*, the fact that the script was written out in advance kept the number of possible changes during filming to a minimum. Other films had similarly short shooting schedules:

12 See the Introduction in which the section on scripting clearly demonstrates controlling tendencies on Robbe-Grillet's part.

> One cannot shoot quickly if one has not written at all. For *Eden and After*, considerable money was involved – Czechoslovakian money, Tunisian money, and French money. I shot the film in two months. For *La Belle Captive*, I shot for three weeks. I must devote more time to preproduction when I know that I have little time to shoot. Therefore, much of *La Belle Captive* was written ahead of time [...] not to write anything at all and to shoot during a very long period of time – for example, six months or a whole year – has great inconveniences. (Ibid.: 124–5)

Conveniently for the writer/director, this strategy helped to limit the chances of actors and crew challenging his autonomy.

Robbe-Grillet's use of the camera, too, is ostensibly dictated by financial as well as artistic considerations. His films display relatively little camera movement, being generally movements of scenes: 'There are three reasons for that. First, I like fixed shots. Second, movement costs money, especially lateral movements. Pans are inexpensive; lateral movements or travelling shots are costly' (ibid.: 125). There is also the need to avoid multiple takes: 'A pan is very likely to be successful; a traveling shot on rails is very likely to fail' (ibid.: 75). In fact, though, his approach to camera movement is also partly determined by the controlling instinct:

> Third, I can better control the work of the technician on a fixed shot because I have regulated the framing at the beginning, and he does not have the right to alter it during the take. Whereas if I explain the movement that he is to make, he may or may not follow my directives well [...] In *L'Immortelle*, I experienced very serious disappointments of this kind [...] Undoubtedly, one of the reasons I have used fewer and fewer shots with the camera in motion is because I do not have total control over the final result. (Ibid.: 125–6)

This economical (in both senses of the word) use of camera can have positive artistic effects. In the case of *Trans-Europ-Express*, for example, the claustrophobia of shooting in a small train compartment transfers itself to the film with success, as Robbe-Grillet himself explains:

> Vous imaginez ce que c'est de tourner dans un compartiment de chemin de fer [...] Il y avait donc [...] trois acteurs, un cameraman, un pointeur et un chef-opérateur; les preneurs de son restaient le plus possible dans le couloir [...] Tout 'naturel' était impossible [...] dans l'ensemble le caractère mal à l'aise et figé du personnage de l'auteur est,

à mon sens, très réussi [...] L'action du film s'est beaucoup embrouillée et le narrateur a tout a fait perdu son fil. Et on voit ces trois person-nages dans leur compartiment qui, alors, sont devenus muets [...] il ne reste plus que leur inutilité. Là c'est vraiment très bien.[13] (Gardies 2005: 138–9)

Control of the camera thus assumes a symbolic function in this film, in which the central conflict is a textual one between a producer/director and his characters. Élias struggles to free himself from the narrative control of a conformist and timorous creator and begins to live his own story, which is much more sexualised than that imposed on him. In this, he is assisted by the beautiful young prostitute, Éva, object of his sado-erotic desires and fantasies, who confuses things further with her own version of his story and hers (Murcia 2005: 49).

A similar tension is represented, Murcia maintains, in *L'Homme qui ment*, in which the three women in the chateau struggle to wrest control of the narrative from Boris, intruding into Boris's story on a narrative level. This first narrative series is interrupted, in alternate shots, by a second in the form of brief shots to begin with (close-ups on a woman's hair), and then more developed scenes such as the scene in which blind man's buff is played which ends up momen-tarily expelling Boris from the fiction and occupying his space and assuming narrative control. Again, woman appears as a ferment of disorder, countering Boris's attempts to establish his autobiograph-ical story, and so constitute himself as a character (ibid.).

Editing

There is one important respect in which Robbe-Grillet is not a new wave film-maker. For Robbe-Grillet as for Eisenstein, the essence of film-making lies in montage, whereas 'the Cahiers du cinéma promoted Bazin's absurd idea [...] that the best film would be a film

---

13 'You can imagine what it is like to shoot in a railway compartment [...] There were [...] three actors, a cameraman, a focus puller and a director of photog-raphy; the sound recorders stayed in the corridor as much as possible [...] Any "naturalness" was impossible [...] on the whole the stiff and ill-at-ease character of the author is very successful in my view [...] The plot of the film is extremely confused and the narrator totally loses track. We see these three characters falling silent in their compartment [...] All that remains is their uselessness. This works very well.'

without montage, since in nature there is no montage. For the New Wave, nature and life were important [...] The great idea of the New Wave was that we have to return to life' (Fragola and Smith 1992: 127).

For Robbe-Grillet, unlike the *Cahiers* group, therefore, film-making depends to a large extent on how images are put together in the editing process, which is partly why he spends much more time on this process than he does on shooting:

> I now insist upon the montage being done not according to what the shots were supposed to be but what they really are. At that moment of discovery the counterpoints, dialectics, and shocks appear that had not been foreseen. I experiment. Experimentation is important in film. If it does not work, then I try something else. I find it essential to insist upon the concreteness of working with film. The same holds true for sounds. With sounds, a scene can change completely during the mixing according to whether we use one tape or another. (Ibid.: 129)[14]

Of the three phases of film-making mentioned above, then, Robbe-Grillet favours the third, relatively inexpensive phase when he and a couple of technicians can work quietly in a studio with an editing machine to put selected shots together. This preference has an artistic as well as a financial rationale. Like the first, scriptwriting phase, the solitary activity of montage offers the director total control. *L'Eden et après*, in fact, and unsurprisingly, given the film's playful structure, was constructed largely during the editing process.[15] Editing, then, was an activity to which Robbe-Grillet devoted a great deal of time and energy. This extended editing process made possible a number of techniques that he found both artistically useful and satisfying. What he calls 'Dysnarrative' is part of a process of challenging and disrupting conventional narrative forms. Robbe-Grillet defines this as follows:

> In film, all it takes is a simple anomalous effect of montage, that of joining two shots one after the other in false continuity to create doubling. I employed that procedure when I shot *L'Immortelle*, which

14 Chateau and Jost develop a theory of montage in their book, *Nouveau cinéma, nouvelle sémiologie*, where they try to conceptualise the montage of Robbe-Grillet's films (1979; Fragola and Smith 1992: 128).

15 This controlling tendency even extends beyond editing to the projection of this film. He was, for example, against the idea of showing the reels of *L'Éden et après* in a different order for every screening. See Chapter 3 for detailed discussion of the film's structure.

can be summarized as follows: false continuity, immobile character, and the character who seems to be in search of himself. (Fragola and Smith 1992: 148)

The scene in *L'Eden* where Violette goes to the factory to meet Duchemin exemplifies this technique. Robbe-Grillet: 'When she is among the storage tanks, she is constantly in false continuity' (ibid.: 149). The effect of this doubling is, as Fragola suggests, that Violette is searching for her own identity (ibid.).

Robbe-Grillet's whole approach to the editing process is therefore based on a rejection of a more traditional 'syntactical' construction of film narrative. He was especially critical of Metz in this regard:

I should add that *Nouveau cinéma, nouvelle sémiologie* opposes the semiology of cinema by Christian Metz. Metz attempted to construct a semiology of cinema, which he called the great syntagmatics, and which was the precise determination of a certain number of cinematographic syntagmas. The underlying criticism that one can make of Metz is that he based his syntagmatics on the novel [...] Chateau and Jost, in opposition to the idea of syntax, which was the grand concept of Bazin and later of Christian Metz, developed the idea of parataxis – that is, the simple juxtaposition of two shots that have no syntactical link. The idea of syntax – one of the great motors of regression in film – immediately made cinema derivative of literature. (Ibid.: 128–9)

The tension between order and disorder, between freedom and control is, then, at the heart of Robbe-Grillet's technical approach to film-making. This tension assumes a metaphorical and symbolic character in the imagery of his films to which we must now turn. While this imagery appears to expose the social, psychological and religious processes of control that lead to the dangers of sexual repression, it also seems to express a preoccupation with the threat of disorder and the need to control this threat. In this regard, dangers associated with the feminine are particularly foregrounded.

Order vs. disorder: objects

Sexual repression is seen as a weapon in the armoury of a fragile order – social, psychological, legal, political – that basic natural instincts are constantly threatening to disrupt. The role and symbolism of objects throughout the novelistic and filmic corpus are on an artistic level closely related to a desire to challenge order, while on a personal and subjective level, these objects also function in ways that may be connected to a desire for a different kind of order.

In the early 1960s, when Robbe-Grillet published his seminal collection of essays, *Pour un nouveau roman*, 'matter', whether in film or in the novel, was both 'étrangère à l'homme et sans cesse en train de s'inventer dans l'esprit de l'homme'[16] (Robbe-Grillet 1963: 127). In this perspective, objects do not bear meaning in themselves but are endowed with it through subjective description, 'dans le mouvement même de la description'[17] (ibid.: 128). Thus, in *Les Gommes*, the tomato, and in *La Jalousie*, the crushed centipede are seen subjectively through the obsession or passion of the character-narrator. Those objects that recur throughout his filmic corpus – broken glass, high-heeled shoe, poisoned drink (magical potion in *L'Eden*), etc. – have a complex set of meanings, not least in relation to an eroticism that is as much authorial in origin as associated with a given character. The very presence of the subjective immediately creates the possibility of bias and control – or absence of control – of any object, whether inanimate or animate. This may be particularly the case in relation to representations of the feminine.

In *Glissements*, some objects (shoe, bottle) are simply observed to be there, while others like the pickaxe or kneeler serve as 'generating objects' (points from which narrative may originate): 'Some are aleatory objects, but others, on the contrary, are related: for example, when the female character says the broken bottle could be a murder weapon' (Fragola and Smith 1992: 74).

Objects, then, may function as symbols and generators of a disorder that is never far below the surface in Robbe-Grillet's work. This disorder is artistically (formally) represented, while at the level of content, the generators that function as stimulants of narrative disorder are also invested with a personal authorial eroticism that sows sexual disorder. For example, the shoe which is seen under a glass globe in *Glissements*, held up as an object of veneration, and clearly possessing religious associations, is also associated with death, lesbianism and prostitution, and as such with disorder in many of its incarnations:

16 'foreign to man and forever inventing itself in man's mind'
17 'in the very movement of description'

It is Claudel's *Satin Slipper*. The woman's shoe is traditionally associated with sin, even in popular tradition. One says, for example, about a woman who sinned that she committed a faux pas. One hears it even in the slang expression 'prendre son pied' (to come). Hence, Buñuel's use of the woman's shoe is a normal association. But in the *Satin Slipper*, the young woman who is afraid of sinning takes off her shoe and puts it on the altar to the Virgin and leaves it there. In the film, the shoe under a glass globe is the one from the *Satin Slipper*. (Ibid.: 80–1)

Objects like the shoe may also be seen in terms of an authorial fetishism, evidence in the text of an unconscious desire to control castration anxiety, fetishes representing, for Freud, an attempt to restore the castrated penis to the woman.[18] The bloody and viscous fluids in these films, a broken bottle or wine glass, the nape of a young woman's neck, a woman's shoe, the doll-like characteristics of his female victims, all these have clear fetishistic potential.[19] Some objects, such as the suitcase in *La Belle captive*, also seem akin in their functioning to those of surrealist art, challenging the logic and linearity of realism, but at the same time, they frequently have an erotic resonance that is identifiable from the author's intertext – Robbe-Grillet of *La Belle captive*: 'It is the same suitcase that was on the back of the bicycle, the same suitcase that the doctor had when he came to declare Corinth dead, the same suitcase that was in the clinic. These suitcases reappear throughout the film, all of which casts a certain shadow on realism. It is Magritte's suitcase as well, from one of his paintings' (ibid.: 109).

The most memorable symbol of fetishism in Robbe-Grillet's cinema, however, is perhaps that of the leather-clad Sara Zeitgeist in *La Belle captive*. Sara's appearance, as she roars along the highway astride a powerfully and phallically thrusting motorbike, has an undeniably fetishistic appeal. Sara on her cycle is also an allusion to the 'angel of death' in Cocteau's *Orpheus* who also rides a motorcycle (ibid.). In Robbe-Grillet's world, eroticism and death are never very far apart.

18 'the fetish is a substitute for the woman's (the mother's) penis that the little boy once believed in and [...] does not want to give up' (Freud: 1977 352).
19 In *Le Voyeur* (1955), Mathias's little girl victim is a living doll. Robbe-Grillet's own avowed interest in young girls may be interpreted in terms of a desire for total control of a sexual kind, a fantasy also present in sadism and necrophilia.

Order vs. disorder: imagery

An authorial expression of the male urge to control manifests itself more subtly in the visual patterns of his fictions. Curves and circles are dominant in the imagery of both novels and films, and are ostensibly intended to suggest resistance to male linearity. At the same time, both have a clear erotic character. In *Marienbad*, as she is pursued by X, A gets lost in the geometrically straight lines and angles both inside the chateau and in the labyrinthine gardens outside. Similar patterns abound in other films: in the city of Istanbul itself in *L'Immortelle* in which Professor N searches in vain for Lale, in the labyrinth of 'conventional clichés' of art, eroticism and violence in *Trans-Europ-Express*, and strikingly, in the café in *L'Eden* which is a labyrinth of mirrors reflecting society's stereotypes. In *Glissements*, the hapless police inspector goes round and round in circles, opening the same doors and trapdoors, searching for clues. Such patterns may represent a female erotic that confuses and confounds male characters. Stoltzfus identifies a progression in Robbe-Grillet's work from a 'conservative, non-sexual imagery' to one 'that many readers and spectators [...] find shocking', from 'the stiff, well-dressed, puppet-like actors in *L'Année dernière à Marienbad*' to 'the women in *Le Jeu avec le feu* whose nude bodies grace a banquet table, an implied cross, or a coffin' (1985: 111). The motivation, Stoltzfus rightly observes, is the parody of repressive societal and religious attitudes and values. But as he also argues, spirals, curves and arabesques are connected in the work with freedom and the feminine, whereas linearity connotes constraint, imprisonment and the masculine: '*L'Immortelle*, for example, contains a dramatic shot of [Lale's] face framed by the spiral configurations of a metal gate. There is a shot of Alice's face in *Glissements progressifs du plaisir* behind the iron spiral of a bed. In *L'Eden et après*, rectangular cages imprison naked women. There is also the celebrated sequence in *L'Eden* of a nude descending a spiral staircase' (ibid.).

What all these examples suggest is an abiding awareness of this tension, one that is central to both the personal or psychological and the collective or political levels of human existence. Such imagery, as we have seen, has already been much commented upon. Less attention has been accorded to another type of image which is particularly common in the films: the necrophilic and its relation to control.

Death, where is thy sting?

Images of death, both borrowed and invented, proliferate in Robbe-Grillet's films, even more so than in the novels. By incorporating such images, the author may be attempting to control death itself, to remove its sting by a process of familiarisation. At the same time, the dead are the only human figures over which it is possible to have complete control. At the erotic level, necrophilia is largely motivated by the possibility to control the desired object, whether woman or man, to have total and unfettered sexual access to it, but it may also be associated with a deep-seated need to exorcise the fear of death by eroticising it.

Among the most striking necrophilic scenes in the films are the figure of the drowned fiancée floating on her back in the sea in *Un bruit qui rend fou*, her breasts clearly visible through her diaphanous dress, echoing Millais's famous painting of Shakespeare's Ophelia floating among the water lilies, Violette wading out into the sea in *L'Eden*, Duchemin in the same film drowned at the foot of the harbour steps in the Bratislava canal and again in Djerba, and Nora in *Glissements* playing in the pools on the beach, pretending to be drowned.[20] For Michel Rybalka, such images are not mere erotic clichés, they are the product of childhood sexual development, indices of a battle between the fascination of alterity and separateness, 'the desire to protect individual boundaries, the fear and fascination of fusion or of death [...] of loss of the self-possessed self [...] The writer fights to stay within the symbolic, in control, but at some level, what tempts him is the limen, regression, and loss' (1986: 35).

A general preoccupation with death is linked aesthetically to the rejection of realist linear chronology, but also, in the straight run to the grave that this chronology implies, to a refusal of mortality itself. In *Marienbad*, the characters exist in a timeless space, as X tries to resurrect events that may or may not have happened in connection with a woman, A, who, in her inability to recall the past or project into the future, has all the characteristics of the living dead. In *L'Immortelle*, *Glissements*, *La Belle captive* and *Gradiva*, dead people live again, and linear chronology is undermined. Robbe-Grillet's films plunge us into a 'présent qui s'invente sans cesse [...] qui se répète, se dédouble, se

20 In the *romanesques*, we encounter Marie-Ange van des Reeves (the ghostly vampire 'fiancée de Corinthe') drowned on a South Atlantic beach, and Robbe-Grillet's own childhood friend, the mysterious Angélique found drowned on his native shores.

modifie, se dément, sans jamais s'entasser pour constituer un passé'[21] (Robbe-Grillet 1963: 133). In *L'Immortelle*, the woman's fleeting appearances throughout the film have a stiffness and lack of movement that suggest a living corpse, especially in repeated shots of her face, eyes wide open and yet otherwise completely still. This impression is reinforced by N.'s passing his hand over her eyes, as if to find out if she is alive. As for death and dead people, there are a number of references, for instance, in the shot of a funeral parade crossing the square in front of the mosque, and in the scene in the graveyard. Burch sees the objective of the film as being to reduce both woman and Orient to the same dead object, a 'necrotic project' summed up in the film's title (2005: 29). On the other hand, these images can equally be read in terms of an attempt to stave off death, N.'s (the narrator's?) project being to bring the phantom-like Lale to life.

Vampirism and necrophilia: cults of life?

The cult of death in the Victorian era is particularly strong, as evidenced in the necrophilic themes of its art and literature. It is as if, no longer sure of an afterlife, the Victorians had decided to cling as long as possible to this one. As an attempt on the physical as well as the symbolic level, a fantasy desire to keep the body alive, however, necrophilia is arguably more a cult of life than of death. The English Pre-Raphaelite artist, Dante Gabriel Rossetti kept his wife's corpse in an open coffin for an entire week in the desperate hope that she was not really dead, and in one of his paintings of her after her death, she has a deathly hue, as if a living corpse. Like Millais's *Ophelia*, Rossetti's wife is represented as suspended between life and death, but crucially on this side of the grave. As a pathological attachment to the body, the necrophilia that haunts these paintings and that Robbe-Grillet echoes in his films is in this sense more accurately defined as an expression of Eros rather than Thanatos. It is also, and for much the same reasons, an expression of a controlling impulse, albeit at the level of play.

The sexualisation of the vampire figure also connects it with Eros. Vampirism is, after all, popularly known as the cult of the undead, or in other words, of the living corpse. For the vampire, blood, the life

---

21 'a present that constantly reinvents itself [...] repeats, duplicates, modifies and contradicts itself without ever solidifying to constitute a past'

force, is an object of desire to be ingested in order to continue to live.

In *Glissements*, blood has a special place, appearing and flowing throughout. Alice apostrophises the priest in the confessional: 'Ecoutez, mon père, le sang qui bat trop fort et demande à sortir ... Ecoutez le flot montant du plaisir que nul amour ne purifie ... Connaissez-vous, mon père, le sang des filles qui jaillit sur la chair blanche en ruisseaux de feu?' [22] (Robbe-Grillet 1974: 136–7). That the blood motif is closely linked to Eros as well as to necrophilia and lesbianism is signposted early in the film. When a girl dies in a fall from a cliff path, A caresses her breasts and kisses her, licking blood off her toe. This gesture is echoed later as A licks red wine off the body of a prostitute, lingering at the corner of A's mouth, cutting to the shot of a man lying in a pool of blood. In a clear parody of the vampire theme, red marks are found on Nora's/lawyer's neck: 'Ce n'est pas du sang, c'est de la peinture rouge' she says to the priest.[23] Alice cuts her foot on a piece of glass and gets the judge to lick her wound (although the blood is not shown, only referred to in the dialogue). Later, the priest kisses A, getting blood on his mouth. The entire film narrative, then, appears obsessed with making blood flow from young women. At the end of the film, Alice tells the lawyer, now Nora: 'Tu n'as plus de sang ... Tu vas mourir ... Tu es belle' (ibid.: 148). [24]

Sado-eroticism and necrophilia are similarly evident in the film's recurrent images of the torture and death of a woman, though the gravity of these images is undermined by surreal shots of a female dummy on an iron bedstead which the girls drag onto a beach. The dummy is streaked with blood and tied to the bedstead, suggesting a parodic intent, but these images are intercut with those of the priest staring as if in erotic fascination. Other such images include those of torture in cellars, with a naked girl bending her neck over a chopping-block, while another naked girl is tortured on a wheel. All are linked to religious repression by the intercutting of shots of the priest in the confessional, A's screams, and the digging of graves, a gesture heavy with symbolism. Another recurrent element in the film, a jagged bottle neck, suggests the image of cutting. During the magistrate's

22 'Father, listen to the blood that is beating so hard and asking to come out... Listen to the mounting flood of pleasure that no love can make pure... father, do you know about the blood of girls that spurts onto white flesh in streams of fire?'
23 'It's not blood, it's red paint'
24 'You have no more blood...you are going to die...you are beautiful'

second visit to Alice in her cell, she breaks a bottle. When she tries to clear it away, it immediately draws blood. The bottle appears in two further scenes, this time filled with red liquid. First, Alice's client, a prostitute, breaks the bottle to pour red juice on to the girl. Then, Alice smears Nora with the juice trapped in the bottle neck, suggesting the spurting of blood.

Sarah Leperchez (2005: 72) suggests that, in the scene in *Glissements* where Alice breaks eggs and smears them on Nora's body, the eggs reinforce the viscous aspect of blood. Sister Julia calls Alice a *fille visqueuse* ('a slimy girl') and a toad (a slimy creature). The idea of the flowing of a liquid and the idea of something sticky, that clings, are associated. In the author's perspective, these motifs are associated with an attack on the revulsion inspired by bodily fluids and above all, by a desire to liberate the feminine, which should be celebrated, not vilified.

Viscosity is a characteristic of blood, and so of the living body, but it is also a quality of what Julia Kristeva identifies as the abject. For Kristeva, all bodily waste and those substances and fluids that the body ejects (blood, vomit, faeces, urine, sweat, etc.) inspire disgust, and yet the abject is not reducible to a particular object, but is rather that which has the quality of being opposed to or outside the self (1980: 9–39). Although Robbe-Grillet does not mention the abject by name, he refers to an earlier theorist's, Gaston Bachelard's analysis. Bachelard's emphasis on the opposition between attraction and revulsion could equally well describe Kristeva's notion of the abject which also depends for its effects on the evacuation of fluids and other bodily substances outside the body.

> AF: What is the function of images such as the mixture of sperm and blood and the raw egg that most people would find disgusting, yet regard with a certain fascination?
> RG: You used the appropriate terms of opposition: for the egg, repugnance and sensuality; for the blood, attraction and revulsion. In each case, a pair of oppositions – attraction and revulsion. That, in effect, is the subject of the film. In particular, viscous material and cutting material are constantly at once opposed and mixed in the film – the broken glass mixed with the viscous red color. Bachelard wrote an entire book on the question. (Fragola and Smith 1992: 61)[25]

25 Bachelard speaks of 'the dynamism established between an attractive image and a repulsive image' (1948: 77).

In *L'Eden*, the heroine liberates herself from this revulsion to sperm, and so from the sexual taboo this revulsion represents, by learning to handle a slimy, sperm-like substance without revulsion.

Robbe-Grillet appears, then, to be challenging the taboos that have traditionally been associated with woman. As a mark of woman's affinity with nature which man fears, blood has for centuries been associated with the control of women by men. On the other hand, this focus on attraction–revulsion with regard to 'abject' substances is partly associated with the vampiric, referred to above as manifestation of a desire to control death, and may also be seen as linked to a wider controlling impulse: with regard to the inside–outside of the body, to physical and psychological responses to other, and above all, to physical attributes of the opposite sex (sperm, blood, both arterial and menstrual, and breast milk, for example). Thus, the abject in Robbe-Grillet's films is to be reincorporated in the body and accepted as an intrinsic part of it, in the same way that fear of the feminine is to be overcome.

La Belle captive

The original title of this 1985 film was *Piège à fourrure* ('Fur Trap'), a title that recalls the fetishism of Sacher-Masoch's *Venus in Furs* and the pleasurable entrapment of men by women. The title eventually settled on was the name given to a famous series of paintings by René Magritte.

The film is based on the Greek legend of the fiancée of Corinth which inspired Goethe's *Elegie* and a chapter of Michelet's *La Sorcière* ('The Witch'). In this legend, a young man falls in love with a pale and fair-haired young woman, and travels to Corinth to ask for her hand in marriage. Her parents are shocked to receive this request, telling him that their daughter has been dead for seven years. However, since the young suitor has made a long journey, they offer him the hospitality of a room for the night. It is, of course, the room of their deceased daughter who appears next to the sleeping man to kill him by sucking all his blood. The fiancée of Corinth is an 'imprisoned soul', a 'beautiful captive' who can never find rest because she herself was murdered. In order to free herself from this curse, she must drink the blood of the living until she finally sucks the life from the man who killed her.

In Robbe-Grillet's reading of the legend, a young man, Walter is given a mission to complete, the precise aim of which he is ignorant: he must take a fur coat containing a message to a certain Van de Reeves who heads a rival organisation. An unforeseen event temporarily distracts him from this mission: he nearly runs over the unconscious body of a pretty young woman, lying in the road. Her thighs are bloodied, her dress torn and her hands tied behind her back. In his attempts to help her, he is caught up in a series of adventures which appear to be unrelated to his mission. Not until it is too late does he discover that these events all play a vital part in it. A second young woman, Sara Zeitgeist, dressed in black leather, sits astride a gleaming motorbike. She is the head of the organisation that has entrusted the hero with his first mission. In a parallel world, she is also his wife. She appears at the beginning of the narrative as a guardian angel protecting the man against all temptations, and she tries to defend him against the 'blonde vampire'. However, all images have their reverse side, and nothing in the narrative can be taken for granted.[26]

In *La Belle captive*, then, as in all of Robbe-Grillet's other films, it is impossible to retrace a coherent story, to distinguish what really happened from what was only dreamt or imagined, and just as the boundaries between the real and the imaginary are blurred, so is that between life and death. Indeed, the notion that beyond the visible world lies another world which exactly resembles our own, but which is false, is a central one in this film. In this imaginary world, all of our actions are replicated. However, Robbe-Grillet suggests, perhaps it is our own world that is false (2005: 697).

Such authorial intentions echo a long pedagogical tradition in literature, most prominent in the *Bildungsroman* of the seventeenth and eighteenth centuries. In tracing the adventures of a young male hero, the narrative also appears to draw broadly on the picaresque tradition, no doubt in part with ironic intent, an effect enhanced by the transparent symbolism of character names such as Sara Zeitgeist and Docteur Morgentodt. The theme of a second dimension clearly resembles the other types of doubling which have been discussed earlier in this book, and which may similarly be inspired by a pedagogical intention. Here, it is given a symbolic expression in

26 For a more detailed summary and discussion of the film narrative and its origins, see Robbe-Grillet 2005: 695–700.

the title painting which the author adapted with the permission of the artist's widow. The main elements of Magritte's work are thus adapted to create a recurrent image in the film: red velvet stage curtains frame a deserted beach, with the ocean in the background; in the foreground in front of the curtains is an artist's easel holding a picture reproducing the sand, the waves and the horizon exactly as they appear in the seascape, as if they were viewed through the velvet curtains. The elements of this 'false' Magritte appear on screen whenever the 'fiancée''s teeth sink into the neck of a victim, as if the vampire's bite brought to life the alternate world framed by the theatre curtains. As the hero gets weaker, he appears to sink deeper into this other world. Is this the staging of his own death? At the end of the film, Walter, executed on the beach, awakens from this nightmare and goes off to work ... to be put to death again in the street outside his flat.[27]

The author's own reading of *La Belle captive* also seems to suggest a desire to make the dead live again. In this film, movement is tellingly from death to life, and not the reverse:

> in *La Belle Captive*, as in 'The Bride of Corinthe', two incompatible worlds coexist: the world of the living and the world of the dead. Between the two [...] a connection is suddenly established, since this young woman comes from the world of the dead and arrives in the world of the living [...] Between the two are what might be called 'locks' as in a canal. When you open the locks, a sudden flow invades completely by the simple fact that an object from another world has entered into this world. It is as if a sudden and enormous flow changed everything. (Fragola and Smith 1992: 106)

Robbe-Grillet also describes the movement from one world to the other in terms of a penetration:

> What interests me in Magritte is the presence on his canvases of several worlds, often of two worlds, that ought not to communicate but connect through an opening. One sees a world that seems real, and in this world, there is an opening. Through this opening, one sees another world. [This] seems to me related to the Greek legend of 'The Bride of Corinth' in which a young man falls in love with a woman who, unbeknownst to him, is dead, is a ghost. My interest in Magritte brought forth a whole series of scenes of going through –

27 Similarly, in *L'Immortelle*, the young woman who has disappeared reappears to die and will disappear again in a car accident. In *L'Homme qui ment*, Boris dies constantly and always comes back to life.

going through a barrier, going through a painting, and so forth; and this relationship obviously recalls the sexual act. (Ibid.: 103)

Fragola comments: 'There is another penetration which is the penetration of Marie-Ange's world as represented by her henchmen who actually enter into Walter's world in order to bring him forcibly back into her world' (ibid.: 106–7).

In the vampiric context, 'to go through' also suggests the piercing of the flesh by the vampire bite and the penetration of the barrier between life and death. These images are strongly erotic, drawing upon the common stereotype of the fictional vampire, popularized in the eighteenth- and nineteenth-century Gothic novel, Bram Stoker's *Dracula* being the best-known example. Even the drink that Walter orders in the bar scene is related to blood and vampirism. Robbe-Grillet explains:

> He asks for a tomato juice and vodka rather than a Bloody Mary. In French the drink is commonly identified by its English name, yet the barman gives it a literal French translation: 'Une Marie sanglante [a Mary who is bloody].' He insists, thereby, on the color of blood [...] this is the first time the theme of blood appears. When 'pale-lipped, she drinks the dark blood-colored liquid',[28] she asks, 'What is this terrible thing?'. Later when you see her in her role as a vampire, on the other hand, she drinks this red liquid with obvious delight. In the Greek legend of 'The Bride of Corinth', the woman drinks the blood of the young men in order to try to take their life force and to live herself. Thus it is hard to know whether she is doing this to draw them into death or to bring herself to life. (Ibid.: 109)

Here, Robbe-Grillet draws attention to the obvious sense in which vampirism, like necrophilia to which it is closely related, may be considered as much a cult of life as of death. Robbe-Grillet's words emphasise the symbolic function of the bite, on one level, although vampirism in general is clearly erotic, a both symbolic and literal mark of sexualised violence. As in *Glissements*, the bloodsucking vampire theme and its related motif of the undead can clearly be linked to an unconscious desire to control both death and an ancient fear of the dead who may return to infect us with their deathly condition.[29]

28 This is an intertextual reference to Robbe-Grillet's 1976 novel, *Topologie d'une cité fantôme* (see Fragola and Smith 1992: 171, n. 2).

29 Sigmund Freud directly links the control of death in human culture to a concomitant fear of the dead (1983 [1913]: 51–63).

La Belle captive is probably the film of Robbe-Grillet's that draws most explicitly on a Gothic tradition that can be seen to have its roots in ancient legend. With the exception of *L'Eden* and its televisual partner, *N. a pris les dés*, it is also, perhaps, the most rigidly structured of his films, its obsessively mathematical structure suggesting a powerful controlling tendency on the part of the author/director.

The film narrative is based on the figure '9', a number that J. E. Cirlot reads as a synthesis of the corporeal, intellectual and spiritual, in other words, as a symbol of totality, itself a notion related to control (1993: 234). Nine episodes are thus precipitated by nine 'signs' or elements in nine different combinations: fur, sticky stain, opening, footsteps, fall, penetration, cries, knife, the noise of running water. Each of these episodes, designed to last on average ten minutes, and so to create a film length of ninety minutes, is announced by nine brief shots.

Total control, or rather its impossibility is, of course, the subject of an anxiety that manifests itself in the film's rigid formal architecture, and the constant slippage of meaning at the level of the plot. These formal structures are in one sense the manifestation of an ineluctable destiny to which the Greek hero was subjected and which Robbe-Grillet cathartically replicates here.

All of the aspects discussed in this chapter are, then, related one way or another to a controlling impulse which may, the evidence suggests, be authorial in origin. The author claims to identify with the feminine figures of his films, but such claims are tendentious. As we have seen in this and the previous chapter, many images of the feminine are associated with a desire for control, which manifests itself both in the rigorously planned textual structures and in the sadism of the imagery (the image of the captive woman being a recurrent one in both the films and the novels). At best, therefore, one can say that there is in Robbe-Grillet's work an ambivalence towards the feminine. This ambivalence may also be associated with the maternal, as may the avoidance of conventional identity labels, which is another characteristic of this author's work.

The rejection of realism may be a rejection, at unconscious levels, of the fixity of the Lacanian Symbolic, just as the embrace of the Imaginary may express a desire to return to the pre-oedipal and undifferentiated relationship with the mother.[30] In a brief passage

30 Julia Kristeva associates the Imaginary with the feminine–maternal (see, for example, Kristeva 1980: 171).

in one of his memoirs, Robbe-Grillet recalls linking an old photograph of his mother with a lost, 'fairy-tale' paradise. The photo is of his mother as a young schoolteacher in Germany, at the Odenwald Schule Oberambach, or OSO: 'Bien entendu, nous nous moquions de maman [...] feignant de croire que l'Oslo était une contrée mythique, fabuleuse, où tout devenait possible mais où personne n'était jamais allé vraiment: *L'Eden*, Cythère, le Monomotapa, *Marienbad*'³¹ (Robbe-Grillet 1987: 115; my emphasis).

For Jacques Lacan, the very nature of desire is a constant slippery quest along an endless chain of signifiers for an object never to be recovered – the lost object of the mother's body. In a Lacanian optic, then, the 'glissements' of Robbe-Grillet's writing as a whole, the slippages of identity that they portray, and above all, the ambivalence towards the feminine–maternal which underlies the sado-eroticism, might be associated at deeper levels with this slippage of desire along the linguistic chain and so with the expression of an anxiety in relation to an unattainable object. This object, represented in his texts by impossible images of female perfection, has nevertheless to be controlled and ultimately destroyed, along with the fears of separation and loss which it embodies. A love–hate relationship with the feminine, expressed as it is in the extreme form of a sado-eroticism which is rendered similarly ambivalent by its ludic presentation, may, in part, at least, then, be the pathological manifestation of an anguish, generated by loss of the maternal object and the death of which this loss is the very first sign and manifestation – anguish which both men and women may recognise. Like all writers and artists, perhaps, Robbe-Grillet's work is, in a more general sense, an attempt to make up for this loss which is also the anguish of all human beings confronted with the void:

> Seule l'œuvre d'art, le texte directement produit par l'angoisse, pourraient ainsi, paradoxalement, échapper pour les siècles des siècles au vide qui les a, eux aussi, mis au monde. Tandis qu'à chaque instant s'effondre devant moi l'univers quotidien, l'écriture de l'imaginaire construit à partir du néant lui-même (pris comme structure) un anti-monde, sur lequel l'angoisse fondamentale ne pourra plus jamais avoir de prise, car c'est cette angoisse précisément – et non pas les

---

31 'Of course, we made fun of mummy [...] pretending to believe that Oslo was a mythical, fabulous country where everything was possible but where no one had ever really gone: *L'Eden*, Cythera, le Monomotapa, *Marienbad*'

mots ou la syntaxe, contrairement à ce que croit le sens commun – qui constituera le matériau dont il est bâti.[32] (Ibid.: 126)

In this sense, one might say that Alain Robbe-Grillet's erotic fantasies speak unconsciously to us all. The films we have been discussing are indisputably written and directed by a man, but they are also about the personal investment of any author in what (s)he writes and the processes of writing and viewing themselves, as much as they are about fantasies that are, in any case, hardly representative of hetero-sexual male desire. As such, these films are accessible to anyone, male or female, with an interest in the intimate and problematic relation-ship between man and woman, between author and work.

References

Bachelard, Gaston (1948), *La Terre et les rêveries de la volonté*, Paris, Corti.

Barthes, Roland (1984), 'La mort de l'auteur', in *Le Bruissement de la langue. Essais critiques IV*, Paris, Éditions du Seuil, 63–9.

Burch, Noël (2005), 'Retour sur *L'Immortelle*', in Prédal, *Robbe-Grillet Cinéaste*, 25–33.

Chateau, Dominique and Jost, François (1979), *Nouveau Cinéma, nouvelle sémiologie: Essai d'analyse des films d'Alain Robbe-Grillet*, Paris, Union Générale d'Éditions.

Cirlot, J. E. *A Dictionary of Symbols* (London: Routledge, 1962; this edition, 1993).

Fragola, Anthony N. and Smith, Roch C. (1992), *The Erotic Dream Machine: Interviews with Alain Robbe-Grillet on His Films* (Southern Illinois University Press).

Freud, Sigmund (1977), Pelican Freud Library 7, *On Sexuality*, Harmond-sworth, Penguin Books.

Freud, Sigmund (1983 [1913]), *Totem and Taboo*, London, Routledge & Kegan Paul.

Gardies, André (1972), *Alain Robbe-Grillet*, Paris, Seghers (Cinéma d'aujourd'hui), 104–25.

Gardies, André (2005), 'Le travail du double', in Prédal, *Robbe-Grillet Cinéaste*, 111–43.

---

32 'Only the work of art, the text directly produced by anxiety, might thus paradoxi-cally escape for all the centuries past and to come from the void that gave birth to them too. While the everyday world collapses in front of me at every moment, the writing of the imaginary constructs an anti-world from the void (as a struc-ture), a world upon which Angst can have no purchase, for it is precisely this Angst – and not the words or syntax, contrary to what common sense dictates – that constitutes the material of which it is made.'

Kristeva, Julia (1980), *Pouvoirs de l'horreur*, Paris, Éditions du Seuil.

Leperchez, Sarah (2005), 'L'orchestration du désordre: une analyse topologique', in Prédal, *Robbe-Grillet Cinéaste*, 67–78.

Murcia, Claude (2005), 'L'image de la femme dans les films d'Alain Robbe-Grillet', in Prédal, *Robbe-Grillet Cinéaste*, 47–55.

Prédal, René (2005), *Robbe-Grillet Cinéaste*, Études publiées sous la direction de René Prédal, Caen, Presses universitaires de Caen.

Ramsay, Raylene (1992), *Robbe-Grillet and Modernity: Science, Sexuality and Subversion*, Gainesville, University Press of Florida.

Ricardou, Jean (ed.) (1976), *Robbe-Grillet, analyse, théorie*, Paris, Union générale d'éditions (10/18), vol. II.

Robbe-Grillet, Alain (1963), *Pour un nouveau roman*, Paris, Éditions de Minuit.

Robbe-Grillet, Alain (1974), *Glissements progressifs du plaisir*, Paris, Éditions de Minuit.

Robbe-Grillet, Alain (1984), *Le Miroir qui revient*, Paris, Éditions de Minuit.

Robbe-Grillet (1987), *Angélique, ou l'enchantement*, Paris, Éditions de Minuit.

Robbe-Grillet, Alain (2005), *Scénarios en rose et noir 1966–1983*, Textes et Photos réunis et présentés par Olivier Corpet and Emmanuelle Lambert, Paris, Librairie Arthème Fayard.

Rybalka, Michel (1986), 'Alain Robbe-Grillet: At Play with Criticism', in Lois Oppenheim (ed.), Lois Oppenheim and Evelyne Costa de Beauregard (trans.), *Three Decades of the French New Novel*, Urbana, University of Illinois Press, 31–43.

Stoltzfus, Ben (1985), *Alain Robbe-Grillet: The Body of the Text*, London and Toronto, Associated University Presses.

TV Degree Zero (1990). Television item on Roland Barthes, made by Illuminations for *The Late Show*, BBC2.

Conclusion

L'art doit être perpétuellement en rupture avec l'art qui le précède immédiatement. (Robbe-Grillet, *Les Lettres françaises*)

Robbe-Grillet's cinema inhabits a very particular world into which realism rarely intrudes. The aged, the very young, the working-class, the uneducated, the ugly are all notable by their absence, and some might regret these omissions, arguing that his films do not deal with 'real-world' issues. On the other hand, absent too are the more shocking manifestations of realism to be found in many contemporary films – the hyperrealistic violence of Tarantino or von Trier, for example. Any violence in Robbe-Grillet's films is never truly realistic, always highly stylised. His is a small world, a world of the interior, characterised by a high degree of selectivity. It is certainly infused with eroticism, and there is plenty of naked female flesh of the 'soft-core' variety, but this is a world of erotic fantasy rather than reality, one largely constructed through a perspective that we have seen to be intensely personal. The erotic scenes from *L'Immortelle* to *Gradiva*, as their author readily admits, are devoid of any of the more messy aspects of sex, which is why he has expressed a distaste for Peter Greenaway's obsession with dirt and decay: 'The scenes that, let us say, involve sticky materials in my films are always very "clean"' (Fragola and Smith 1992: 135). In Julia Kristeva's terms, the abject is almost completely absent, the one possible exception being a 'pretend' viscous fluid in *L'Eden*, in a scene that points ironically to the very distaste it is ostensibly designed to conjure away. This curious scene seems to constitute a *mise en abyme* of the tension we have seen to exist throughout this study between Robbe-Grillet's oft-stated description of art as an exploration of form, and the intensely personal contents of his films.

To his credit, Robbe-Grillet accepted that this tension existed from the 1980s onwards, retrospectively acknowledging its presence even in the early novels. While it may not surprise us to hear that *Le Voyeur* was inspired by the author's sexual fantasies, even a novel as apparently formalistic as *La Jalousie*, he confessed, contains elements from personal fantasy and his own reality. Like the tides of the Atlantic ocean that formed the backdrop of his childhood, the personal returns. As Maurice Blanchot so acutely observed, this 'ressassement éternel' is doubtless a universal human condition. We are all continually constructing ourselves, since childhood, through narrative. In a Freudian perspective, some of these narratives are reassuring, and indeed necessary if we are to take our part in society, but many other narratives, those of our dreams and nightmares, can prove persistently disturbing. The role and value of all art is in no small measure to help us deal with our anxieties in the face of a mortality we all share, and as Octavio Paz avers, the erotic in art has a special place in this process:

> l'érotisme [...] est une expérience totale, mais qui ne se réalise jamais totalement, car son essence est un perpétuel *au-delà*. Le corps étranger est un obstacle ou un pont: dans un cas comme dans l'autre il faut le franchir. Le désir, l'imagination érotique, la voyance érotique traversent les corps, les rendent transparents. Ou les anéantissent. Au-delà de toi, au-delà de moi, par le corps, dans le corps, par-delà le corps, nous voulons voir *quelque chose*. Telle est la fascination érotique, qui m'arrache à moi-même et me conduit vers toi. Ce qui me fait aller au-delà de toi. Nous ne savons pas de science exacte ce que c'est, sauf qu'il s'agit de quelque chose *en plus*: plus que l'histoire, plus que le sexe, plus que la vie et la mort.[1] (1994: 28–9)

This close association between sex and death, one to which Georges Bataille has drawn attention more than any other author in the twentieth century, may help us to understand the unconscious need for control – mastery of the one may help to master the other. It is

1 'the erotic [...] is a total experience, but one which is never completely realised, for its essence is a perpetual *beyond*. The foreign body is an obstacle or a bridge: in either case it has to be crossed. Desire, the erotic imagination, the erotic gaze go through the body, rendering it transparent. Or else they destroy it. Beyond you, beyond me, by virtue of the body, in the body, beyond the body, we want to see *something*. Such is the fascination of the erotic which tears me away from myself and leads me to you. Which in turn makes me go beyond you. We do not know exactly what it is, except that it is something *more*: more than history, more than sex, more than life and death.'

the overriding paradox of these films that, on the one hand, they exhibit a controlling drive, and on the other, demand the spectator's active participation in a difficult cinema, the interest of which very largely resides in the intellectual challenge it poses to its audience. All of the films, as we have seen, are on one important level games in which the spectator is invited to take part, games that, like the Nim game in *Marienbad*, can be lost and won at the same time, games that, like Freud's 'Fort! Da!', help the player to come to terms with the absence and loss of a primary erotic object that, for the male at least, will be the model for all others. In all of his work – novels, essays, memoirs, as well as films – Robbe-Grillet invites us to question all received wisdoms, to go beyond the surface image, beyond self and other, searching for *something*, something more, more than history, sex, life or death.

Since Robbe-Grillet's own death in February 2008, it has become possible to hasard a summation of the importance of his work and its influence. The evaluation of influence is always a precarious business, but one which this study, completed two years after his death, cannot avoid. It is probably wise to be brief here, and I shall, in any case restrict my comments to the impact of his films.

Insights may occasionally be had from reading critics hostile to the author in question. In Jean-Philippe Domecq's recent book on Robbe-Grillet, for example, the author draws attention to the self-contradictions of an author/film-maker promoting objectivity who finally admitted in the 1980s that everything he wrote was about himself. Domecq's criticisms may be thought not entirely fair in that they imply that the artist's thought does not evolve with the experience of age and changing intellectual ideas and fashions. As we have seen, Robbe-Grillet was largely reacting in his early years against a humanist-inspired literary movement, dominated by the existentialist philosophies of Sartre and Camus. Domecq also critiques the emphasis on form at the expense of content, on what this critic sees as novelty for its own sake, and the opposition to all that went before. There is nothing new here, and yet, such criticisms do help to focus our attention on what has endured into the new millennium.

Robbe-Grillet's influence on artists of the 1950s onwards has already been well documented, for instance, Roy Lichtenstein's work with the flatness of the comic book, and the sculptures of Robert Morris which one critic describes as 'simply existing' (Domecq 2005:

90). Others have noted possible influences in Peter Greenaway's cinema – *The Cook, the Thief, His Wife and Her Lover* (1989) – and there are arguably echoes of Robbe-Grillet's eroticism in the work of David Lynch and of Pedro Almodóvar, but perhaps his most important contribution to cinema is more general than that to be found in specific films.

Robbe-Grillet's desire to 'build the world anew' ironically implies a *reprise*, an orphic glance backwards that necessarily engages him constantly in the literary and artistic past. In this, he is a product of the post-war years, and his work, while proclaiming itself as 'nouveau', is unavoidably trapped in a conversation which now seems largely irrelevant. Realism, in the cinema at least, is actually pretty rare in a contemporary Hollywood which is currently dominated by sci-fi fantasy, disbelief-suspending romcoms, and a renewal of the vampire fetish, while the best-known examples of world cinema, such as that of Almodóvar, the Coen brothers, and even Tarantino, fizz to a greater or lesser degree with a magic realism that is a long way from the old, Balzacian models of narrative that Robbe-Grillet so denigrates. French cinema itself appears divided between the continuation of a trend towards similar forms of fantasy begun in the 1990s (*Y aura-t-il de la neige à Noël?* (1996), *Amélie* (2001)), and a return to socio-political realism (most recently, for example, *Entre les murs* (2008)). These themes are not new but an extension or reprise of earlier cinematic themes – old wine, sometimes, in new bottles. The positive side of this trend is a frank recognition that all human art is repetitious at its core, implying an invigoration of those powerful stories that we never tire of reading. In this sense, Robbe-Grillet's cinema is, both outside and within itself, a re-engagement with age-old and deepseated human concerns.

Robbe-Grillet's view of the future of film was a deeply pessimistic one:

> Dominated by capitalist concentration of the machinery of production and the machinery of distribution, the American system is now in the process of invading Europe. Also, the shrinking movie audience especially contributes to the decline of the cinema [...] Intellectual curiosity has disappeared [...] The European public will be responsible for this débâcle, exactly in the way in which the American public is responsible for the silliness of American film. (Fragola and Smith 1992: 162–3)

This view was expressed in 1992. It is depressing to note just how much it still holds true now. At the same time, and in spite of the commercial imperatives that even more so now, determine the nature of most films made worldwide, it is in the healthy encouragement to re-evaluate the role of the third art as an intellectual medium that Robbe-Grillet's most valuable and most influential legacy can be found. In his unique attempts to renew cinematic forms and in the eternally relevant questions about sexuality and the self that his work poses, the not insignificant corpus of Robbe-Grillet's filmic œuvre represents a lasting contribution to experimental and avant-garde cinema.

References

Domecq, Jean-Philippe (2005), *Alain Robbe-Grillet?*, Paris, L'Esprit des pénin-sules.

Fragola, Anthony N. and Smith, Roch C. (1992), *The Erotic Dream Machine: Interviews with Alain Robbe-Grillet on His Films*, Carbondale and Edwards-ville, Southern Illinois University Press.

Paz, Octavio (1994), *Un au-delà érotique: le marquis de Sade*, Paris, Éditions Gallimard.

Filmography

L'Année dernière à Marienbad (1961), 94 min., 35 mm, b/w

Franco-Italian co-production
Screenplay: Alain Robbe-Grillet
Direction: Alain Resnais
Cast: Delphine Seyrig, Giorgo Albertazzi, Sacha Pitoeff, Françoise
Bertin, Luce Garcia-Ville, Héléna Kornel, Françoise Spira, Karin
Toeche-Mittler, Pierre Barbaud, Wilhelm Von Deek, Jean Lanier,
Gérard Lorin, Davide Montemuri, Gilles Quéant, Gabriel Werner
Production: Précitel, Terrafilm
Distribution: Cocinor

L'Immortelle (1963), 90 min., 35 mm, b/w

Franco-Italian co-production.
Screenplay: Alain Robbe-Grillet
Executive producers: Samy Halfon, Michel Fano
Direction: Alain Robbe-Grillet
Photography: Maurice Barry
Editing: Bob Wade
Sound: Michel Fano
Music: Georges Delerue and col. de mus. Turques
Cast: Françoise Brion (L, Lâle, Leyla, etc.), Jacques Doniol-Valcroze
(N), Guido Celano (M, man with dogs), Ulvi Uraz (antique dealer),
Catherine Robbe-Grillet (Catherine Sarayan), Belkis Mutlu (maid),
Sezer Sezin (Turkish woman)
Production: Tamara Films, Como Films, Cocinor (Paris), Dino de
Laurentis Cinématografica (Rome)
Distribution: Cocinor

Trans-Europ-Express (1966), 90 min., 35 mm, b/w

Franco-Belgian coproduction
Screenplay: Alain Robbe-Grillet
Executive producer: Samy Halfon
Direction: Alain Robbe-Grillet
Photography: Willy Kurant
Editing: Bob Wade
Sound designer: Michel Fano
Sound engineer: Raymond Saint-Martin
Music: Verdi
Cast: Jean-Louis Trintignant (Élias, himself), Marie-France Pisier (Éva, herself), Alain Robbe-Grillet (Jean, the director), Catherine Robbe-Grillet (Lucette, the script girl/continuity person), Charles Millot (Franck), Christian Barbier (Inspector Lorentz), Daniel Emilfork, Henri Lambert (the false policeman), Nadine Verdier (chambermaid), Clo Vanesco (cabaret singer), Paul Louyet (Marc, the producer), Raoul Guyland (an intermediary), Prima Symphony (stripper)
Production: Como-Films
Distribution: Lux CCF

L'Homme qui ment (1968), 95 min, 35 mm, b/w

Franco-Czechoslovakian co-production
Screenplay: Alain Robbe-Grillet
Executive producer: Samy Halfon
Direction: Alain Robbe-Grillet
Photography: Igor Luther
Editing: Bob Wade
Sound adviser: Michel Fano
Sound engineer: Raymond Saint-Martin
Cast: Jean-Louis Trintignant (Boris), Yvan Mistric (Jean Robin), Sylvie Bréal (Maria), Sylvia Turbova (Sylvia), Zuzana Kocurikova (Laura), Dominique Prado (Lisa), Josef Kroner (Frantz), Catherine Robbe-Grillet (the chemist), Josev Cierney (the father), Dusan Blaskovic (innkeeper), Bada, Julius Vasek (members of the Resistance)
Production: Como-Films, Lux CCF (Paris), Ceskoslovensky Film (Bratislava)
Distribution: Lux CCF

L'Eden et après (1971), 100 min., 35 mm, col. (Eastmancolor)

Franco-Czechoslovakian co-production, with Tunisian assistance/
 participation
Screenplay: Alain Robbe-Grillet
Executive producer: Samy Halfon
Direction: Alain Robbe-Grillet
Photography: Igor Luther
Editing: Bob Wade
Sound designer: Michel Fano
Sets: Anton Krajcovic
Cast: Catherine Jourdan (Violette), Pierre Zimmer (Duchemin-
 Dutchman), Lorraine Rainer (Marie-Ève), Sylvain Corthay (Jean-
 Pierre), Richard Leduc (Marc-Antoine), Juraj Kukura (Boris),
 Ludwik Kroner (Frantz), Yarmila Kolenicova (the suicide), Cathe-
 rine Robbe-Grillet (the professor), Franz Gerva (the new waiter)
Production: Como-Films (Paris), Ceskoslovensky Film (Bratislava)
Distribution: Plan Films

N. a pris les dés (1971; broadcast in 1975 on FR3), 35 mm, TV film,
col. (Eastmancolor)

ORTF-Como-Films co-production
Cast: as for *L'Eden et après,* with Catherine Jourdain (as Elle), Richard
 Leduc (as N.), Pierre Zimmer (as the stranger)
Producers : as for *L'Eden et après*

Glissements progressifs du plaisir (1974), 35 mm, 105 min., col.
(Eastmancolor)

French production
Screenplay: Alain Robbe-Grillet
Executive Producers: André Cohen, Marcel Sebaoun
Direction: Alain Robbe-Grillet
Photography: Yves Lafaye
Editing: Bob Wade
Sound designer: Michel Fano
Cast: Anicée Alvina (Alice), Olga Georges Picot (Nora, Maître David
 the lawyer), Jean-Louis Trintignant (the police inspector), Michael
 Lonsdale (the magistrate), Jean Martin (the priest), Marianne
 Egerickx (Claudia), Claude Marcault (Sister Julia), Nathalie Zeiger
 (Sister Maria), Maxence Mailfort (the client), Bob Wade (the grave-

digger), Humbert Niogret (the photographer), Catherine Robbe-Grillet (a nun), Alain Robbe-Grillet (a passerby)
Production: Coséfa Films, SNETC
Distribution: Fox

Le Jeu avec le feu (1975), 35 mm, 109 min., col. (Panavision–Anamorphic–Eastmancolor)

Franco-Italian co-production
Screenplay: Alain Robbe-Grillet
Executive producer: Georges Dybman
Assistant director: Hubert Niogret
Direction: Alain Robbe-Grillet
Photography: Yves Lafaye
Editing: Bob Wade
Sound: Jack Jullian, Jean-Philippe Leroux
Music: Musical adaptations of *Il Trovatore* (Verdi), *Erica* (German march) and *Carolina* (Chico Buarque) by Michel Fano
Cast: Jean-Louis Trintignant (Franz and Francis), Philippe Noiret (Georges de Saxe), Anicée Alvina (Caroline de Saxe), Philippe Ogouz (Pierre Garin), Agostina Belli (Maria, the de Saxes's maid), Sylvia Kristel (Diana van den Berg), Christine Boisson (the woman in the trunk), Nathalie Zeiger (Tania), Martine Jouot (Erica), Serge Marquand (Mathias), Jacques Seiler (taxi driver), Jacques Doniol-Valcroze (Inspector Laurent)
Production: Arcadie Films (Paris), Madeleine Films (Paris), Cinecompany (Rome)
Distribution: UGC–CFDC

La Belle captive (1983), 90 min., 35 mm, col. (Eastmancolor)

French production.
Screenplay: Alain Robbe-Grillet
Executive producer: Bernard Bouix
Direction: Alain Robbe-Grillet
Assistant directors: Richard Malbequi, Jeanne Biras, Marianne Chouchan
Photography: Henri Alekan
Sets: Aimé Deude
Editing: Bob Wade
Co-adaptation and direction of the video sequence: Frank Verpillat

Sound: Gérard Barra

Music: Schubert's *Fifteenth Quartet*, 'The Mooch', by Duke Ellington

Cast: Daniel Mesguich (Walter Raim), Gabrielle Lazure (Marie-Ange van de Reeves), Cyrielle Claire (Sara Zeitgeist), Daniel Emilfork (Inspector Francis), Roland Dubillard (Prof. van de Reeves), François Chaumette (Dr Morgentodt), Gilles Arbona (the barman), Arielle Dombasle (the hysterical woman), Jean-Claude Leguay (the cyclist), Nancy van Slyke (the waitress), Denis Foucray (the valet), Michel Auclair (narrator)

Production: Anatole Dauman, Argos Films, FR3

Distribution: Argos Films

Un bruit qui rend fou/The Blue Villa (1995), 100 min., col. (CinemaScope, Dolby Stereo SR)

Belgian–French–Swiss co-production

Screenplay: Alain Robbe-Grillet

Executive producer: Jacques de Clercq

Assistant directors: Paul de Ruijter, Nikos Giannopoulos, Jérôme Paillard

Direction: Alain Robbe-Grillet and Dimitri de Clerq

Assistant director: Denis Seurat

Photography: Hans Meier

Sets: Alain Chennaux

Editing: France Duez

Sound: François Musy

Music: Nikos Kypourgos, 'Ballad of Senta', sang by Arielle Dombasle

Cast: Fred Ward (Frank), Arielle Dombasle (Sarah-la-Blonde), Charles Tordjman (Nord), Sandrine Le Berre (Santa), Dimitri Poulikakos (Thieu), Christian Maillet (father), Muriel Jacobs (Kim), Michalis Maniatis (Mars)

Production: Nomad Films (Brussels), Euripide Productions (Paris) and CAB Productions (Lausanne)

Distribution: Studio des Ursulines

C'est Gradiva qui vous appelle (2006), 118 min., col. (Dolby SRD)

Franco-Belgian co-production

Screenplay: Alain Robbe-Grillet

Direction: Alain Robbe-Grillet

Photography: Dominique Colin

Editing: France Duez
Costumes: Claire Gérard-Hirne
Sets: Daniel Bevan
Sound: Jean Minondo, Philippe Baudhuin
Technical adviser: Yves Hanchar
Cast: James Wilby (John Locke), Arielle Dombasle (Gradiva/ Hermione), Dany Verissimo (Belkis), Farid Chopel (Anatoli), Marie Espinosa (Claudine), Lofti Yahya Jedidi (the beggar), Farida Khelfa (Elvira), Mehdi Ouazzani (Inspector Mahdi)
Production: Acajou Films
Coproduction: Z Company, Les Films du Lendemain
Distribution: Zootrope Films

Select bibliography

A great deal has been published about Robbe-Grillet's work, including the cinema, since the early 1960s and I recommend below only those publications which are likely to prove both useful and accessible to the reader of this book. These include the four *cinéromans*, *L'Année dernière à Marienbad*, *L'Immortelle*, *Glissements progressifs du plaisir* and *C'est Gradiva qui vous appelle*, indispensible for readings of the four films in question.

Alain Robbe-Grillet, Œuvres Cinématographiques (1982), Édition vidéocritique, Paris, Ministère des Relations Extérieures, Cellule d'animation culturelle. An indispensible but now difficult to access collection on videocassette of *L'Immortelle*, *Trans-Europ-Express*, *L'Homme qui ment*, *L'Eden et après* and *Glissements progressifs du plaisir*. The collection also includes interviews on cassette by François Jost with the author-director. Transcripts of the latter and a number of short essays by other critics are available in an accompanying booklet.

Armes, Roy, *The Films of Alain Robbe-Grillet* (1981), Purdue University Monographs in Romance Languages, vol. 6, Amsterdam, John Benjamin B.V. A comprehensive and accessible study of the films of the 1960s and 1970s.

Chateau, Dominique and Jost, François (1979), *Nouveau Cinéma, nouvelle sémiologie: Essai d'analyse des films d'Alain Robbe-Grillet*, Paris, Union Générale d'Éditions. An interesting semiotic analysis of the films. Given its date of publication, it does not cover *La Belle captive* (1983), *Un bruit qui rend fou* (1995) and *C'est Gradiva qui vous appelle* (2006).

Deleuze, Gilles (1985), *Cinéma 2: L'Image-temps* (Paris: Minuit); English edition: Deleuze, Gilles (1989), *Cinema 2: The Time Image*, London, Athlone Press. A highly theoretical but often brilliantly illuminating study of post-war French cinema which contains numerous references to Robbe-Grillet's films up until the mid-1980s, focusing on the representation of time.

Domecq, Jean-Philippe (2005), *Alain Robbe-Grillet?*, Paris, L'Esprit des péninsules. A rare example of hostile criticism, this book contains few references to the films, but usefully challenges a critical consensus which has been largely sympathetic to Robbe-Grillet.

Fragola, Anthony N. and Smith, Roch C. (1992), *The Erotic Dream Machine: Interviews with Alain Robbe-Grillet on His Films*, Carbondale and Edwardsville, Southern Illinois University Press. A unique and extremely useful collection in English of interviews with the author, dealing exclusively with the films.

Freud, Sigmund (1985 [1919]), 'Das Unheimliche'; trans. 'The Uncanny', Harmondsworth, Middlesex, Pelican Freud Library 14: *Art and Literature*, Penguin Books, 335–76. Freud's essay is relevant to the strange, dreamlike aspects of the films.

Freud, Sigmund (1985 [1907]), 'Delusions and Dreams in Jensen's *Gradiva*', in *Art and Literature*, Harmondsworth, Middlesex, Pelican Freud Library 14, Penguin Books, 27–118. Directly relevant to *C'est Gradiva qui vous appelle*.

Higgins, Lynn A. (1996), *New Novel, New Wave, New Politics: Fiction and the Representation of History in Postwar France*, Lincoln and London, University of Nebraska Press. An excellent overview of the new novel and new cinema, Higgins's book is particularly useful for an understanding of *L'Année dernière à Marienbad*.

Mulvey, Laura (1975), 'Visual Pleasure and Narrative Cinema', *Screen* 16:3, 6–18. Mulvey's seminal essay on voyeurism is indispensible in any analysis of the erotic elements of the films.

Prédal, René (ed.), *Robbe-Grillet Cinéaste*, Presses universitaires de Caen, 2005. A rare volume of essays focusing exclusively on the films, including the projected *C'est Gradiva qui vous appelle*.

Ramsay, Raylene (1992), *Robbe-Grillet and Modernity: Science, Sexuality and Subversion*, Gainesville, University Press of Florida. Well written and often illuminating, if rather disorganised study of the novels and films, Ramsay's study is exceptional in combining both sympathetic and at times critical approaches.

Robbe-Grillet, Alain (1963), 'Temps et description dans le récit d'aujourd'hui', in *Pour un nouveau roman*, Paris, Éditions de

Minuit, 123–34. An early essay by Robbe-Grillet, touching on the treatment of time in the novel and cinema.

Robbe-Grillet, Alain (1987), *Angélique, ou l'enchantement*, Paris, Éditions de Minuit. The second of the 'romanesques', or fictional autobiographies, this volume contains many references to those films made up to the mid-1980s.

Robbe-Grillet, Alain (2005), *Préface à une vie d'écrivain*, Paris, France Culture, Éditions du Seuil. Spoken commentaries by Robbe-Grillet on his work. The last two chapters focus on the films.

Robbe-Grillet, Alain (2005), *Scénarios en rose et noir 1966–1983*, Textes et photos réunis et présentés par Olivier Corpet and Emmanuelle Lambert, Paris, Librairie Arthème Fayard. An invaluable resource for any study of the films of the 1960s and 1970s, including detailed summaries and shooting-scripts by the author.

Saïd, Edward W. (2003 [1978]), *Orientalism*, London, Penguin Books. Directly relevant to a post-colonial reading of *L'Immortelle*, *L'Eden et après*, and *C'est Gradiva qui vous appelle*.

Stoltzfus, Ben (1985), *Alain Robbe-Grillet: The Body of the Text*, London and Toronto, Associated University Presses. An excellent and very accessible study of the author's work, containing many references to the filmic corpus up to the late 1970s.

Van Wert, William F. (1977), *The Film Career of Alain Robbe-Grillet*, London, George Prior Publishers. Though limited to the films of the 1960s and 1970s, this is a useful reference work, containing synopses and an exhaustive and detailed list of critical studies up to 1976.

Wilson, Emma (2005), 'Material Relics: Resnais, Memory and the Senses', *French Studies*, 59:1, 25–30. A brilliant and informative reading of *L'Année dernière à Marienbad*.

The *cinéromans*

Robbe-Grillet, Alain (1961), *L'Année dernière à Marienbad*, Paris, Les Éditions de Minuit.

Robbe-Grillet, Alain (1963), *L'Immortelle*, Paris, Éditions de Minuit.

Robbe-Grillet, Alain (1974), *Glissements progressifs du plaisir*, Paris, Éditions de Minuit.

Robbe-Grillet, Alain (2002), *C'est Gradiva qui vous appelle*, Paris, Éditions de Minuit.

Index